SHAKESPEARE'S

MACBETH

Other books in the Christian Guides
to the Classics Series:

Bunyan's "The Pilgrim's Progress"

Dickens's "Great Expectations"

Hawthorne's "The Scarlet Letter"

Homer's "The Odyssey"

Milton's "Paradise Lost"

SHAKESPEARE'S

MACBETH

LELAND RYKEN

CROSSWAY

WHEATON, ILLINOIS

Cover illustration: Howell Golson

Cover design: Simplicated Studio

First printing 2013

Printed in the United States of America

Unless otherwise indicated, Scripture quotations are from the ESV® Bible (*The Holy Bible, English Standard Version®*), copyright © 2001 by Crossway. 2011 Text Edition. Used by permission. All rights reserved.

Trade paperback ISBN: 978-1-4335-2612-1
PDF ISBN: 978-1-4335-2613-8
Mobipocket ISBN: 978-1-4335-2614-5
ePub ISBN: 978-1-4335-2615-2

Library of Congress Cataloging-in-Publication Data

Ryken, Leland.
   Shakespeare's Macbeth / Leland Ryken.
      p. cm.— (Christian guides to the classics)
   Includes bibliographical references.
   ISBN 978-1-4335-2612-1 (tp)
   1. Shakespeare, William, 1564-1616. Macbeth. 2. Shakespeare, William, 1564-1616—Religion. 3. Christianity and literature.
I. Title.
PR2823.R95   2013
822.3'3—dc23   2012025866

Crossway is a publishing ministry of Good News Publishers.

BP		23	22	21	20	19	18	17	16	15	14	13
15	14	13	12	11	10	9	8	7	6	5	4	3	2	1

Contents

127057

The Nature and Function of Literature

We need to approach any piece of writing with the right expectations, based on the kind of writing that it is. The expectations that we should bring to any work of literature are the following.

The subject of literature. The subject of literature is human experience, rendered as concretely as possible. Literature should thus be contrasted to expository writing of the type we use to conduct the ordinary business of life. Literature does not aim to impart facts and information. It exists to make us share a series of experiences. Literature appeals to our image-making and image-perceiving capacity. A famous novelist said that his purpose was to make his readers *see*, by which he meant to see life.

The universality of literature. To take that one step further, the subject of literature is *universal* human experience—what is true for all people at all times in all places. This does not contradict the fact that literature is first of all filled with concrete particulars. The particulars of literature are a net whereby the author captures and expresses the universal. History and the daily news tell us what *happened*; literature tells us what *happens*. The task that this imposes on us is to recognize and name the familiar experiences that we vicariously live as we read a work of literature. The truth that literature imparts is truthfulness to life—knowledge in the form of seeing things accurately. As readers we not only look *at* the world of the text but *through* it to everyday life.

An interpretation of life. In addition to portraying human experiences, authors give us their interpretation of those experiences. There is a persuasive aspect to literature, as authors attempt to get us to share their views of life. These interpretations of life can be phrased as ideas or themes. An important part of assimilating imaginative literature is thus determining and evaluating an author's angle of vision and belief system.

The importance of literary form. A further aspect of literature arises from the fact that authors are artists. They write in distinctly literary genres such as narrative and poetry. Additionally, literary authors want us to share their love of technique and beauty, all the way from skill with words to an ability to structure a work carefully and artistically.

Summary. A work of imaginative literature aims to make us see life accurately, to get us to think about important ideas, and to enjoy an artistic performance.

Why the Classics Matter

This book belongs to a series of guides to the literary classics of Western literature. We live at a time when the concept of a literary classic is often misunderstood and when the classics themselves are often undervalued or even attacked. The very concept of a classic will rise in our estimation if we simply understand what it is.

What is a classic? To begin, the term *classic* implies the best in its class. The first hurdle that a classic needs to pass is excellence. Excellent according to whom? This brings us to a second part of our definition: classics have stood the test of time through the centuries. The human race itself determines what works rise to the status of classics. That needs to be qualified slightly: the classics are especially known and valued by people who have received a formal education, alerting us that the classics form an important part of the education that takes place within a culture.

This leads us to yet another aspect of classics: classics are known to us not only in themselves but also in terms of their interpretation and reinterpretation through the ages. We know a classic partly in terms of the attitudes and interpretations that have become attached to it through the centuries.

Why read the classics? The first good reason to read the classics is that they represent the best. The fact that they are difficult to read is a mark in their favor; within certain limits, of course, works of literature that demand a lot from us will always yield more than works that demand little of us. If we have a taste for what is excellent, we will automatically want some contact with classics. They offer more enjoyment, more understanding about human experience, and more richness of ideas and thought than lesser works (which we can also legitimately read). We finish reading or rereading a classic with a sense of having risen higher than we would otherwise have risen.

Additionally, to know the classics is to know the past, and with that knowledge comes a type of power and mastery. If we know the past, we are in some measure protected from the limitations that come when all we know is the contemporary. Finally, to know the classics is to be an educated person. Not to know them is, intellectually and culturally speaking, like walking around without an arm or leg.

Summary. Here are four definitions of a literary classic from literary experts; each one provides an angle on why the classics matter. (1) The best that has been thought and said (Matthew Arnold). (2) "A literary classic ranks with the best of its kind that have been produced" (*Harper Handbook to Literature*). (3) A classic "lays its images permanently on the mind [and] is entirely irreplaceable in the sense that no other book whatever comes anywhere near reminding you of it or being even a momentary substitute for it" (C. S. Lewis). (4) Classics are works to which "we return time and again in our minds, even if we do not reread them frequently, as touchstones by which we interpret the world around us" (Nina Baym).

How to Read a Story

Macbeth, like the other classics discussed in this series, is a narrative or story. To read it with enjoyment and understanding, we need to know how stories work and why people write and read them.

Why do people tell and read stories? To tell a story is to (a) entertain and (b) make a statement. As for the entertainment value of stories, it is a fact that one of the most universal human impulses can be summed up in the four words *tell me a story*. The appeal of stories is universal, and all of us are incessant storytellers during the course of a typical day. As for *making a statement*, a novelist hit the nail on the head when he said that in order for storytellers to tell a story they must have some picture of the world and of what is right and wrong in that world.

The things that make up a story. All stories are comprised of three things that claim our attention—setting, character, and plot. A good story is a balance among these three. In one sense, storytellers tell us *about* these things, but in another sense, as fiction writer Flannery O'Connor put it, storytellers don't speak *about* plot, setting, and character but *with* them. *About what* does the storyteller tell us by means of these things? About life, human experience, and the ideas that the storyteller believes to be true.

World making as part of storytelling. To read a story is to enter a whole world of the imagination. Storytellers construct their narrative world carefully. World making is a central part of the storyteller's enterprise. On the one hand, this is part of what makes stories entertaining. We love to be transported from mundane reality to faraway places with strange-sounding names. But storytellers also intend their imagined worlds as accurate pictures of reality. In other words, it is an important part of the truth claims that they intend to make. Accordingly, we need to pay attention to the details of the world that a storyteller creates, viewing that world as a picture of what the author believes to exist.

The need to be discerning. The first demand that a story makes on us is surrender—surrender to the delights of being transported, of encountering experiences, characters, and settings, of considering the truth claims that an author makes by means of his or her story. But we must not be morally and intellectually passive in the face of what an author puts before us. We need to be true to our own convictions as we weigh the morality and truth claims of a story. A story's greatness does not guarantee that it tells the truth in every way.

Mr. WILLIAM
SHAKESPEARES
COMEDIES,
HISTORIES, &
TRAGEDIES.

Published according to the True Originall Copies.

Martin Droeshout sculpsit London

LONDON
Printed by Isaac Iaggard, and Ed. Blount. 1623.

Title page of the book in which
Macbeth was first published.

Macbeth: The Play at a Glance

Author. William Shakespeare (1564–1616)

Nationality. English

Date of composition. 1606

Approximate number of pages. 100 in a paperback edition

Available editions. Numerous, including Pelican, Arden, Ignatius, Dover Thrift, Signet, Norton, Oxford University Press

Genres. Drama; tragedy; murder story

Setting for the story. Scotland in the eleventh century

Main characters. Macbeth, who aspires to be king of Scotland and commits a murder to obtain the throne; Lady Macbeth, who shares her husband's political ambitions; King Duncan, murdered by Macbeth; Banquo, Macbeth's military companion whom Macbeth murders in his ascent to the throne; Macduff, who brings Macbeth to justice

Plot summary. As the story begins, Macbeth is a loyal servant of King Duncan of Scotland, fighting in support of the king to put down a rebellion. As Macbeth is returning to Duncan's castle, he has his ambitions for the kingship fueled by prophecies from three witches. When King Duncan later visits Macbeth's castle, Macbeth and Lady Macbeth murder him and thereby secure the throne. But the Macbeths are guilt-haunted by their evil actions and begin to unravel psychologically. Lady Macbeth becomes dysfunctional, and Macbeth becomes more and more violent in his paranoia over imagined rivals to the throne. A resistance to Macbeth gains momentum under the leadership of Macduff, whose forces defeat Macbeth in open battle. At the end of the play, Duncan's son Malcolm, rightful heir to the throne, is established as king. The main plotline is a story of crime and punishment.

Structure. (1) The usual three-phase pattern of a story of crime and punishment: the antecedents of the crime (what led up to it), the occurrence of the crime, the consequences of the crime. (2) The six-phase pattern that tragedies follow (see page 13 for details). (3) A prolonged conflict between good and evil, with evil seemingly unconquerable in the first half of the play but then gradually being defeated by forces of good. (4) A design known as the well-made plot: exposition (background information, showing Macbeth's noble character and position in relation to the king); inciting moment (Macbeth's meeting with the witches); rising action (Macbeth's resolving the conflict between his moral conscience and his political ambition in the wrong direction); turning point (our hearing about an army being mustered to defeat Macbeth); further complication (Macbeth fights a losing battle against guilt and the opposing army); climax (Macbeth's defeat on the battlefield); denouement (tying up of loose ends, with Malcolm being installed as king of England).

Cultural context. Shakespeare is a Renaissance writer, and as such he is indebted to two great intellectual and cultural movements from the past. One is the classical tradition, to which it is common to attach the term *humanism*. Two principles of classical humanism are especially important in *Macbeth*: (1) the key to virtuous behavior is to have one's reason control the appetites and emotions; (2) the entire universe constitutes a great chain of being ruled by God; the well-being of all people and kingdoms consists of maintaining this divinely ordained order (e.g., citizens need to submit to their rulers, wives to their husbands, emotions and appetites to reason). The Reformation went hand in hand with the Renaissance. We can see its presence in *Macbeth* in an abundance of biblical references, in the assumption of a Christian worldview, in its ethical system (its system of virtues and vices), and in its doctrinal viewpoints (e.g., Christian ideas about sin, damnation, heaven, hell, good, and evil are embodied in the action).

Place in Shakespeare's canon. *Macbeth* is the last of Shakespeare's "great tragedies"; its predecessors were *Hamlet, Othello,* and *King Lear.* One-time poet laureate of England John Masefield called *Macbeth* "the most glorious" of Shakespeare's plays, and literary critic Oscar Campbell said that it is "the greatest treasure of our dramatic literature."

Shakespeare's language. Shakespeare possessed the largest vocabulary of any English writer—over 21,000 words (compared with 13,000 for John Milton and 6,000 for the King James Bible). Much of Shakespeare's language is archaic for modern readers. Additionally, Shakespeare's plays are highly poetic. All of this makes Shakespeare's plays difficult to read or hear in performance. Three good rules to follow are these: (1) read slowly; (2) make use of the notes in your chosen edition of the play; (3) operate on the premise that no one understands all of Shakespeare's words and lines, and that you can enjoy and understand *Macbeth* even though many of the words and metaphors are beyond your grasp.

Tips for reading or viewing. (1) Macbeth requires a balancing act between paying attention to the poetry and to the story. We cannot have an in-depth experience of the play without doing justice to both the poetic and narrative qualities. (2) Image patterns are so important in Shakespeare's plays that they become "actors" in the plays. Image patterns in *Macbeth* include light and darkness, hand imagery (with multiple meanings), disease imagery, blood, and sleeplessness. (3) The play is rich in atmosphere, and virtually all of it is spooky and foreboding. (4) This play is the most famous literary portrayal of the psychology of guilt; Shakespeare shows the spiritual as well as the mental and emotional effects of guilt.

The Author and His Faith

The myth of the secular Shakespeare is a fallacy foisted on us by an unbelieving age. Before we look at the plays, we need to consider the cultural milieu in which Shakespeare lived. Shakespeare's England was a thoroughly Christian and Protestant society. The Bible was the best-selling book. Regular church attendance was mandatory (and there are no parish or civil records that suggest that Shakespeare was found guilty of nonattendance). Shakespeare was baptized in the local Anglican church. Upon his retirement he became a lay rector (also called lay reader) in that same church. When he died he was buried inside the church (not in the surrounding cemetery). All of this should predispose us to expect Christian elements in Shakespeare's plays.

One evidence of this pervasive Christianity in Shakespeare's plays is the abundance of biblical allusions and echoes. At least two thousand biblical references exist, and additional biblical parallels and subtexts keep surfacing. Additionally, the plays assume the same kind of reality that the Bible does: the existence of God and Satan, heaven and hell, good and evil. There is nothing in Shakespeare's plays that shows skepticism about the basic doctrines of the Christian faith. Storytellers show their intellectual allegiances in the world that they create within their stories; the world of Shakespeare's plays is a thoroughly Christian world (as well as classical).

The particular form that Christianity takes in Shakespeare's plays is specific to the genres (with comedy and tragedy giving voice to quite different aspects of the Christian faith) and to the individual plays. Here is a list of leading ideas in *Macbeth*, and the list is entirely congruent with Christianity: (1) the power of evil in the individual soul; (2) the destructive effects of evil on those who do it and on society; (3) the importance of obeying hierarchy at every level where it exists (including the individual, family, and state); (4) the necessity for people to choose between good and evil, and the moral responsibility that attaches to the choices that people make; (5) the reality of guilt; (6) the sanctity of human life and the horror of murder; (7) the reality of moral temptation; (8) the certainty of justice, with evil ultimately punished and good rewarded; (9) a view of the person as having the dual potential for good and evil.

It is easy to find biblical stories, poems, proverbs, and didactic (teaching) passages in the Bible that assert these same things. The fact that some of the ideas also belong to other religious systems does not make them any less Christian. Christianity was the only active belief system in England in Shakespeare's day, and the version of these ideas that Shakespeare embraced was the Christian version.

The Two Main Genres of *Macbeth*

Drama

Drama belongs to the broader category of narrative or story, so everything that is said earlier in this guide about how to read a story applies to *Macbeth*. But drama has its own way of telling a story:

- The action is not stated directly by a storyteller or narrator; instead we need to piece together the action by listening to the dialogue of characters. The portrayal is objective in the sense that our only basis for interpreting action, scene, and character is what we hear characters in the play say. We have to come to the right interpretations without the help of a narrator who directs our responses.
- Instead of being divided into chapters the way a novel is, plays are divided into acts and scenes. The movement from one scene or episode to the next is much more abrupt than the smooth flow found in a novel or short story.
- The strong point of drama is not plot but the presentation of characters and clashes between them.
- Because *Macbeth* falls into the further category of *poetic* drama, we need to pay even more attention to the words that we read or hear than we usually do when reading a story.

Tragedy

Tragedy holds an esteemed place in literature. A good definition of tragedy is that it tells the story of a hero who begins in an exalted position, makes a tragic choice in which he or she displays a tragic flaw of character, and as a result of this tragic choice is plunged into catastrophe and suffering. The plotline of a tragedy is a fall from prosperity to catastrophe, with particular emphasis on the tragic choice of the protagonist. The main attention of a literary tragedy falls on the characterization of the tragic hero, including a tragic flaw of character. Tragedies follow a six-phase sequence, as follows:

- An opening dilemma in which the protagonist is drawn in two directions, one good and the other bad.
- The hero's tragic choice between the forces competing for his or her soul.
- The catastrophe that engulfs the tragic hero, stemming directly from the tragic choice.
- The suffering that accompanies the catastrophe.
- A moment of tragic perception near the end where the hero expresses insight into what he or she did wrong.
- The death of the tragic hero.

Tragedy presupposes a high view of the person. Part of this high view is the premise that people are endowed with a power of choice. Additionally, we are expected to see the ways in which the tragic hero is representative of people generally, including ourselves.

Shakespeare's Theater

While most dramatic performances of Shakespeare today are based on modern theatrical conventions (including realistic stage props), a few performances adhere to Renaissance practices. These Renaissance stage conventions are worth knowing about, partly for the interest of the matter, and partly to make us aware of what is non-Shakespearean in most of the performances that we view. Here is a thumbnail sketch of what play going was like in Shakespeare's London.

- All plays were held in the afternoons in outdoor theaters that had no lighting.
- The theaters were round or octagonal amphitheaters. The circumference of this structure had three tiers of seats, all of which were under a roof.
- In the middle was an unroofed area known as the pit, where people who paid a small entrance fee *stood* for the entire performance of two-to-three hours.
- The entire physical experience thus resembled attendance at an athletic event in a stadium more than play attendance by night at an indoor theater.
- Jutting out into the pit on one side was the stage, with a roofed area and rooms behind curtains at the back side of the stage.
- The entire physical arrangement noted above explains why it is called "theater in the round."
- All players were male actors; female roles were played by males.
- Because changes of scenes in the plays were almost always accompanied by shifts in setting as well, very few stage props were used. Shakespeare often built descriptions into his lines to take the place of physical stage props.
- Costumes were elaborate and costly.
- Shakespeare's audiences loved noise and music, so there were frequent trumpet flourishes, banging of drums, and gunpowder blasts.
- The whole cross-section of the population attended plays, from aristocrats to uneducated "groundlings" who stood in the pit.

From all that has been said, it is obvious that the biggest gap between Renaissance and modern theatrical conventions centers on realism (life-likeness). The Renaissance did not expect realism in its plays. They expected tragedies to be in poetic form, for example. Modern realistic performances of Shakespeare's plays are different from the plays as originally conceived. This does not make them illegitimate; Shakespeare's plays are remarkably universal and adaptable. Some performances even place the action in different times and places than what Shakespeare conceived. These should be recognized as adaptations, part Shakespearean and part something else.

ACT 1, SCENE 1

Plot Summary

A storm on a remote Scottish heath. This brief opening scene of just eleven lines grabs the attention of the audience and sets an atmosphere of darkness and demonic evil that will persist to the very end of the play. On a desolate heath, to the accompaniment of thunder and lightning, three witches agree to meet after the storm and greet Macbeth, returning from a battle, before sunset. In unison they chant, "Fair is foul, and foul is fair," and then depart.

Commentary

A leading function of opening scenes like this is to introduce us to the "world" of the work. Even a statement like "fair is foul, and foul is fair" packs an enormous weight of meaning: the world of the play is a world of false appearances and inverted values (fair should be fair, foul should be foul).

In Shakespeare's day witches were believed to exist, but the age did not agree on their nature. The rival views were that they were women in communion with the Devil, or actual demons disguised as human witches, or humans under the power of Satan and used for his purposes. Their purpose was to do evil things to people and tempt them to do evil things themselves. Shakespeare never tips his hand on what he believes to be true about witches, but this is unimportant. The important point is that Shakespeare's witches are fictional inventions that image forth a true reality, namely, the action of supernatural evil in the world. We should not get caught up in speculation about what witches might or might not be in real life but

Plays in Shakespeare's London were performed in the afternoon in outdoor theaters. Shakespeare accordingly had to grab the attention of a milling and noisy audience without benefit of dimming the lights or an announcement over a loudspeaker. The stage directions for the opening scene here call for "thunder and lightning," which were produced by flashes of gunpowder. This practice was not without its hazards: in 1613 the Globe Theater caught fire and burned down during a performance of Shakespeare's *Henry VIII*, having been set on fire when powder charges from two cannon shots landed on the thatched roof of the theater, and actors and spectators escaped with difficulty.

instead concentrate on the reality of which they are metaphors.

For Reflection or Discussion

What features of the world of the play are introduced right at the outset? In a play that is much praised for its atmosphere, what atmosphere is established? What view of evil is implied by its embodiment in supernatural creatures? What foreshadowing is established in this brief opening scene?

ACT 1, SCENE 2

Plot Summary

The military camp of King Duncan. The entrance of the tragic hero, Macbeth, is delayed for another scene, but this scene indirectly introduces us to Macbeth as he is discussed by the king and others in his camp. King Duncan has found it necessary to meet two threats to his kingdom. The first, a rebellion led by Macdonwald, has been put down by Duncan's great generals Macbeth and Banquo. Second, when the Norwegians, taking advantage of the rebellion, launched an attack on Scotland, Macbeth met the threat, defeating the Norwegians and capturing the traitorous Thane of Cawdor, who had sided with the Norwegians. Duncan announces that he will bestow the rebel's title on Macbeth and orders Ross to go and greet Macbeth as Thane of Cawdor.

An early example of a biblical allusion in a play that has many of them occurs at line 40: "Or memorize another Golgotha." This is a *metaphoric* reference to the place of Christ's crucifixion; its meaning is something like "make the place memorable as another place of death."

Commentary

This scene serves two functions: to establish the political situation that is the context of the action, and to characterize Macbeth. Macbeth becomes so villainous as the play unfolds that we tend to forget that before he can be a tragic hero who undergoes a fall he needs initially to be a person with good qualities.

The scene also establishes the political world of the play (and of Shakespeare's tragedies generally). In that world, power resides with the king and his army. The heroes in such a society are the rulers who can govern a nation and the warriors who can win battles for the king. One further dimension fits here as well: within the great chain-of-being framework, in which virtue consisted of keeping one's place in the hierarchy, there was a particular phobia about treason to the ruling monarch and the civil chaos that rebellion against authority brought. Although Macbeth does not heed the implied warning, his very defeat of the rebellious Thane of Cawdor foreshadows what he himself is about to reenact when he rebels against his king.

For Reflection or Discussion

The contribution of the scene to the plot is obvious, so we should concentrate on the characterization of Macbeth. Even though he has not yet entered the play, we are given a lot of preliminary information about him as we listen to the dialogue between Duncan and the messengers from the battlefield. What are the elements in this early portrait of the tragic hero that idealize him and establish him in an exalted position from which a tragic fall is possible?

ACT 1, SCENE 3

Plot Summary

A desolate heath. First we listen to the three witches talk about the mischief they have most recently performed. When Macbeth and Banquo come into view returning from battle, the witches utter three prophecies about Macbeth's political future and then three riddling prophecies about Banquo's future. After the witches vanish into thin air, the king's messengers Ross and Angus arrive to announce Macbeth's new title, Thane of Cawdor. Macbeth ironically foreshadows his whole career when he asks why the messengers dress him in "borrowed robes."

Beginning at line 116, Macbeth moves in and out of a trancelike reverie in which his consciousness is split between inner musing and dialogue with the other characters. The key action is the inner monologue, in which Macbeth makes clear that he expects to be king. He even imagines the act of killing the king to usurp the throne. But in the very act of imagining a murder, Macbeth is horror-struck, as he refers to his hair being unfixed and his heart knocking at his ribs. The imagery delivers a double message, as Macbeth is torn between an impulse to do something evil and his conscience, which deters him from doing the evil deed.

Commentary

The opening dialogue among the three witches mainly establishes an atmosphere of the grotesque and unearthly. One of the functions of witches in the Renaissance view is that they tempt humans to their ruin. That is their function here, based on the upward political career predicted for Macbeth

Shakespeare never actually calls his witches by that title, instead referring to them as "the weird sisters." *Weird* is a loaded word here: it not only calls attention to the witches' unnatural and grotesque qualities and habits, but it is an implied reference to an important Old English word and concept known as *Wyrd*, meaning "fate."

from Thane of Glamis (which Macbeth already was when the action began), to Thane of Cawdor (which he is about to become), to king (which Macbeth quickly assumes to be inevitable). The witches make three ambiguous or riddling prophecies to Banquo, the gist of which is that Banquo will beget kings though he himself will not be king.

Macbeth is startled by the witches' predictions, but at the same time he has an unhealthy and ominous fascination with them (we should note that his key statements begin with stressed one-syllable words that seem blurted out, such as "Stay . . ."; "Tell . . ."; "Speak . . ."). As the action unfolds, it is obvious that in the space of just a few lines the first two agents of temptation (two of an eventual four) have begun to work upon Macbeth's ambition—his rising political fortunes and the supernatural prophecies of the witches.

Once the witches utter their prophecies, we enter the rising action phase of the plot. In this play it can be formulated as a conflict between Macbeth's ambition and the obstacles that deter him from giving his ambition free rein. The chief initial obstacle is the hero's healthy conscience. Macbeth is not a villain at this phase of the story; he is a person of strong conscience tempted to do an evil deed.

> Fate actually plays an extremely small role in this play. Macbeth is not forced to do anything against his will. In keeping with the Christian premises of this play, Macbeth is a free moral agent who chooses evil over good. The only element of fate is that Macbeth is singled out for unusual testing. The witches provide *the occasion for* Macbeth's tragic choice, but they do not compel it. The biblical subtext that informs this play is James 1:14–15: "Each person is tempted when he is lured and enticed by his own desire. Then desire when it has conceived gives birth to sin, and sin when it is fully grown brings forth death."

For Reflection or Discussion

The action is again straightforward, so we should concentrate on Macbeth, the tragic hero, as he is subject to temptation. Where can we see or infer that Macbeth is undergoing a temptation? Macbeth's moral conscience is set over against his ambition; where do we see evidence of his healthy conscience at work within him? The quickness with which Macbeth assumes that he will be king leaves us to decide whether he has long harbored that ambition or whether the witches' prophecies suddenly plant that possibility in his mind; what is your impression?

ACT 1, SCENE 4

Plot Summary

Either King Duncan's camp or his palace. The main external action is that Macbeth meets King Duncan for the first time in the play, following a brief dialogue between the king and his son Malcolm regarding the traitorous and now dead Thane of Cawdor. The king commends Macbeth, publicly announces that his son Malcolm is next in line for the throne, and invites himself to Macbeth's castle at Inverness. In Macbeth's brief soliloquy ("aside") we can see his ambition grow before our eyes.

Commentary

If we "read between the lines," it is obvious that the temptation of ambition takes a giant leap in this scene. Macbeth's rising political fortunes (he is named Thane of Cawdor, in fulfillment of the witches' second prophecy) feed his desire to reach for the kingship. His brief soliloquy (lines 48–51) makes this explicit, as he sees Malcolm's being named heir apparent to the throne as an obstacle to be overcome.

For Reflection or Discussion

How does the conversation between Malcolm and Duncan about the treason, repentance, and death

---

Malcolm, the king's son, reports that the traitorous Cawdor has died penitently and calmly (lines 3–11). Duncan, in turn, muses on the inability to read a person's character by appearance (lines 11–14). He no more than utters that sentiment than Macbeth enters ("Enter Macbeth," the stage direction reads ominously), as if to signal that a new cycle of treachery is ready to begin.

This play is saturated with passing references to aspects of Christian doctrine and experience. While such references do not by themselves prove a Christian allegiance to the play (something that can be proved by the ideas affirmed in the play), they demonstrate the extent to which the characters in the play, and Shakespeare as playwright, operate with Christian beliefs and experiences as the habitual furniture of their minds. In the picture of the Thane of the previous Thane of Cawdor serve as a foil (parallel and contrast) to the career of the *next* Thane of Cawdor (Macbeth)? Where do we catch the clues that Macbeth's temptation continues on an upward trajectory? Playwrights love the technique of dramatic irony in which the audience knows something of which at least some characters in the play are ignorant; where do we see dramatic irony in this scene?

of Cawdor's repentant death, we catch a glimpse of the penitent who confesses his sin and dies at peace. We can then contrast this to how the next Thane of Cawdor (Macbeth) eventually dies.

ACT 1, SCENE 5

Plot Summary

Inside Macbeth's castle. The scene opens with Lady Macbeth reading a letter that she has received from her husband about his meeting with the witches. Lady Macbeth responds with a speech built on three notable motifs. (1) She begins by declaring that her husband will most definitely "be / What thou art promised," that is, king. (2) Then she expresses a fear that her husband's personality is such that he will be unable to execute the king to gain the crown. (3) Given the problem of Macbeth's inability to carry out the murder, Lady Macbeth ends the speech by declaring her intention to browbeat her husband ("chastise with the valor of my tongue") into going through with the murder.

Lady Macbeth's musings are interrupted by the arrival of a messenger, who announces that King Duncan will visit the castle this very night. Lady Macbeth is nearly beside herself with planning the execution of the king. She prays to "spirits / That tend on moral thoughts," presumably demonic agents, to overpower her human weak-

In addition to direct biblical allusions in *Macbeth*, we are continuously reminded of biblical stories that function as a subtext in Shakespeare's story. Lady Macbeth becomes a latter-day Jezebel as she repeats what Jezebel did in the story of Naboth's vineyard (1 Kings 21). She is a wicked queen who urges and plans a crime to help a husband-king who is himself too weak to grab something he wrongfully desires.

ness and make her capable of performing the murder. Darkness imagery establishes an atmosphere of evil and foreboding.

When Macbeth enters the room, Lady Macbeth immediately appeals to his sense of ambition. The scene ends with husband and wife making veiled references to murdering the king.

Commentary

Lady Macbeth is obviously the last and greatest of the agents of temptation that help tip the scales in the dilemma faced by the tragic hero—a struggle between ambition and conscience that by himself he could never resolve. The role of Lady Macbeth in this scene (and in the first half of the play) is a familiar archetype (recurrent motif in literature and life): she plays the role of temptress. We are led to feel how horrible life will be around the Macbeth household if Macbeth does not go through with the murder.

But Macbeth is also tempted from within by his own ambition. This is clear from the letter that he sent to his wife, which she reads at the beginning of the scene. Macbeth speaks of having "burned in desire to question [the witches] further" and of having "stood rapt in wonder." Additionally, he speaks of his wife as "my dearest partner of greatness," showing that he assumes that he will become king.

One of the most interesting aspects of Lady Macbeth's soliloquy (her words spoken before Macbeth enters) is the portrait she paints of her husband. She verbalizes what the entire first half of the play dramatizes: Macbeth's ambition leads him to want to usurp the throne, but his moral conscience (which Lady Macbeth regards

This play contains no fewer than thirty-seven images of hell and demons. The play thus agrees with biblical and Christian teaching that evil is not merely earthly and human but spiritual as well. Exploring what the Bible says about demons and supernatural agents of evil will fill out the picture of what is happening in the play.

as a weakness) prevents him from grabbing the kingship.

This is another scene that drips with dramatic irony. When Lady Macbeth says that the messenger "brings great news" in regard to the king's arrival, she is thinking about the sudden opportunity to kill the king. When Macbeth replies to the question of when the king intends to depart, he says, "Tomorrow, as he purposes," and we can see the hidden meaning that the king may not do "as he purposes" at all. When Lady Macbeth says that the visiting king "must be provided for," the statement does not carry its usual meaning of extending hospitality but a sinister meaning of being put to death. And so forth.

For Reflection or Discussion

Based on Lady Macbeth's assessment of her husband's character and personality, how well would you say she knows her husband? What details show the dynamics of Lady Macbeth's temptation of her husband? What details hint at the fact that Lady Macbeth is intent on committing a crime that is beyond her human capability of performing? At what points do we thrill to the dynamics of dramatic irony? Where do we catch hints that as husband and wife become partners in crime they have been drawn closer together as a couple?

ACT 1, SCENE 6

Plot Summary

Macbeth's castle. In a Shakespearean play, some brief scenes exist solely for the purpose of setting

This scene achieves depth of field beyond the foreground action by the inclusion of biblical elements. The idealization that Duncan heaps on the Macbeth castle is heightened with the statement of "the temple-haunting martlet," an allusion to Psalm 84:3, with its picture of the sparrow that has found a home in the temple. Furthermore, the sense of impending betrayal is handled in such a way as to make us think of Judas's betrayal of Jesus (literary critics would speak of the Judas story as a subtext for this scene in the play).

up the next main event. This is one of those scenes. It is devoted to Duncan's arrival at the Macbeth castle, making possible the murder that is about to occur. With the convergence of the king's party (including his sons) at the castle, the ingredients are in place to allow the Macbeths to perform their nighttime murder.

Commentary

This scene of warm welcome is permeated with dramatic irony. Irony is present in the opening lines in which Duncan extravagantly praises the pleasantness and welcoming atmosphere of the castle. Irony is present at the end when Duncan says to Lady Macbeth, "Give me your hand. / Conduct me to my host [Macbeth]; we love him highly."

For Reflection or Discussion

The world that Shakespeare creates in this play is a thoroughly Christian world; what details in this scene contribute to the Christian world of the play? What biblical allusions and echoes are present? The literary forms that storytellers introduce into their portrayal of human experience serve the function of highlighting the content; how does the pervasive dramatic irony in this scene heighten our sense of betrayal in the Macbeths' murder of the king?

ACT 1, SCENE 7

Plot Summary

Macbeth's castle. With the king now positioned in Macbeth's castle, this scene is devoted to the Macbeths' preparing themselves mentally for the murder. The scene begins with another famous soliloquy in which Macbeth calculates the reasons he should not murder Duncan, only to end with his resolve to murder the king. Macbeth's words, which take us inside his very mind as he contemplates committing murder, reinforce his calculating temperament.

Then Lady Macbeth enters the room. She responds to Macbeth's provisional conclusion that "we will proceed no further in this business" by browbeating him into agreeing to commit the murder. Lady Macbeth is obviously the greatest of the four agents of temptation that push Macbeth into the murder (the other three agents are the witches' prophecies, Macbeth's rising political fortunes, and Macbeth's inner ambition).

Commentary

Macbeth's soliloquy in which he tallies up the reasons for not killing Duncan serves multiple functions. It takes us inside the criminal's mind and shows us how calculating he is. Further, it is obvious to us and to Macbeth that he should not commit the murder and in fact cannot escape getting caught, and yet he goes on with the murder, showing that the murder is an irrational act and also that Macbeth's inclination to evil and his ambition for the kingship are so great that they completely overpower his reason. Also, Macbeth shows insight into his character when he ends by saying that the only thing propelling him to the murder is his "vaulting [leaping] ambition."

The scene ends with Macbeth giving in to temptation ("I am settled, and bend up / Each corporal agent to this terrible feat"). Macbeth is no moral weakling, however. He gives in to the temp-

In lines 2–7 Macbeth theorizes that committing the assassination would pose no difficulty to him if only he could be assured of success in this life ("here upon this bank and shoal of time"). In fact, he is so thoroughly the earth-bound humanist at this moment that he is willing to "jump [risk] the life to come," meaning that he is willing to risk eternal damnation in the life to come. Here is one of many places in the play where the Christian framework of damnation and salvation is the assumed worldview.

Shakespeare's plays are replete with pictures of dysfunctional families. In this play Shakespeare portrays how *not* to conduct a marriage relationship, as Macbeth and Lady Macbeth spur each other on in evil. We can profitably ponder what the Bible encourages by way of influence of one spouse on another. If Shakespeare's play shows how negatively one spouse can influence another, what is the positive ideal? As just one example, the virtuous wife of Proverbs 31 "does [her husband] good, and not harm, all the days of her life" (v. 12).

As Macbeth begins to weaken under his wife's relentless pressure, he asks, "If we should fail?" His resistance to the murder has degenerated into a merely practical question of whether he and his wife can succeed with the murder. Lady Macbeth tells him to "screw your courage to the sticking point." This is a reference to archery—specifically to the act of drawing the string taut (sometimes with the aid of a cranking device) until the arrow was caught in a notch ("sticking point"), ready to be shot.

tation only after agonizing within himself, and the scene itself is structured as a rhythm of vacillation between the drive of ambition and the hero's moral conscience. Although Macbeth loses his battle with temptation to evil, it would be wrong to say that he has killed his conscience. His conscience will continue to plague him until a much later point in the play.

Lady Macbeth's characterization also advances in this scene. In her dialogue with Macbeth, her speeches are several times longer than the speeches of Macbeth. At this early point in the play the initiative in evil lies with Lady Macbeth.

An additional level of meaning is the breakdown of hierarchy within the family that we witness. The Renaissance worldview placed a premium on hierarchy of authority, which was believed to exist on cosmic, state, family, and individual levels. In this scene we witness a breakdown of family structure as Macbeth allows himself to be dominated by his wife. Of course the more crucial factor is that Lady Macbeth stands for the wrong thing morally and that she works to destroy another person's soul.

For Reflection or Discussion

What are the multiple things that make up Macbeth's frame of mind as he moves toward committing the murder? The same question applies to Lady Macbeth: as we listen to her browbeat her husband, what do we learn about her mindset in regard to killing the king? Additionally, Lady Macbeth undertakes a persuasive strategy for counteracting Macbeth's momentary statement that the murder is off; what arguments does she use to overpower her husband? A classic question applied to this play is why we sympathize with the tragic hero; upon reflection, at what points in this scene do you find a sympathetic bond between Macbeth and yourself? At what moments do we see a moral conscience pulling Macbeth in the right direction? The key to doing justice to this scene is to scrutinize Macbeth carefully. What psychological forces are at work within him? What real-life counterparts have you known? What details further establish the world of the story as a Christian world?

ACT 2, SCENE 1

Plot Summary

Macbeth's castle at midnight. Macbeth's fellow general Banquo is about to retire for the night. He meets Macbeth in the hallway, and the two converse briefly. As usual, Macbeth plays the role of the complete liar when he tells Banquo that he does not think about the prophecies of the witches.

When Macbeth is alone, he utters another of his famous soliloquies. As in the soliloquy in the preceding scene, this one again shows us Macbeth's state of mind as he approaches the murder. The most notable aspect of the soliloquy is that it expresses Macbeth's hallucination, as he imagines a bloody dagger before him leading him to the king's chamber. It is no surprise that this scene is known as "the dagger scene." Just when we think that Macbeth will shrink back from the terrible act, a bell rings, and he suddenly steels himself to do the deed ("I go, and it is done").

In the final two lines of the scene, Macbeth says that the bell that sounds the turn of the hour summons the soon-to-be-dead Duncan "to heaven, or to hell." This once again brings into our consciousness the Christian scheme of salvation and damnation, and the assumption that heaven or hell is the eternal destination of every person. The world of the imagination that we enter as we assimilate this play is a thoroughly Christian world.

Commentary

Macbeth is the classic study of guilt in English literature (its counterpart in American literature being *The Scarlet Letter*). Five scenes, in particular, are governed by the psychological and spiritual dynamics of guilt. Here is the first of the five. We infer that Macbeth's hallucination is the product of his guilt-haunted mind, just as in real life people often lose their grip when what they are about to do (or have already done) is some horrible deed.

ACT 2, SCENE 2

Plot Summary

Macbeth's castle, just after the murder. This is one of Shakespeare's great scenes. It is commonly called "the murder scene." Although it is true that this is the scene where we relive the murder, strictly speaking the action consists of what takes place immediately after the murder has been committed.

The first thing we learn is the details regarding how the murder went and the logistics of attempting to cover it up. Despite her big talk, Lady Macbeth had to take the stimulant of wine before she could go through with the murder: "That which hath made them drunk hath made me bold." Lady Macbeth drugged the bedtime drink of the guards so they would sleep through the murder. Things are tense, but we momentarily think that the crime can succeed.

Things begin to deteriorate when Macbeth enters the bedroom where Lady Macbeth is standing, straining to catch a sense of how the murder has gone. Macbeth is unnerved by what he has

Lady Macbeth claims that she herself would have committed the murder "had [Duncan] not resembled / My father as he slept." This statement cuts two ways: on the one hand we see a touch of humanity in Lady Macbeth at the point of greatest moral breakdown; on the other hand we picture the murdered king as helpless, benign, and fatherly, increasing our revulsion at the murder of him.

done. He looks at his bloody hands and declares it to be "a sorry sight." In effect he wakes up from a nightmare and finds it a reality. Throughout the remainder of the scene Macbeth is a deranged person, buckling under the strain of having committed a murder. He hallucinates and hears accusing voices. By contrast, Lady Macbeth keeps her composure and manages to put the bloody daggers near the sleeping grooms as incriminating evidence. Interspersed knockings at the gate of the castle late in the scene heighten the tension.

Commentary

On the level of plot, the key to organizing this scene is to analyze how Macbeth and Lady Macbeth are foils or contrasts to each other. Macbeth crumbles under the strain, while Lady Macbeth is like a composed housewife tidying up the house. Additionally, Macbeth perceives the guilt and moral pollution that attaches to the murder, while Lady Macbeth is without moral perception in the matter.

Macbeth is a murder story and follows the familiar conventions of the genre, beginning with the story of Cain and Abel (Gen. 4:1–16). The physical details of the murder are always part of the genre, as well as the evocation of the horror of murder. Murder stories are also suspense stories, as we are led to wonder if the murderers will "get away with" the murder. All of these dynamics are in full force in this scene. In popular literature, we remain at the level of the physical, but with great writers like Shakespeare the story of physical murder is only the basis for exploring serious moral issues and significant human experience.

One of Shakespeare's celebrated effects in the play is the interspersed knockings that occur in the

Macbeth's behavior in this scene is rich in its psychological realism. In today's language, Macbeth hallucinates and is delusional (he sees and hears purely imaginary phenomena in his mind), and he dissociates (enters a sphere of consciousness completely unrelated to the physical situation in which he finds himself).

Two important images appear in the scene: sleeplessness as the sign of the guilty soul or guilty conscience, and the bloody hand. An additional striking example of poetry is the string of metaphors Shakespeare composed to describe sleep at lines 36–40. The lines are so striking that they are often quoted out of their context in the play as a poetic meditation on sleep. But in their context here they are actually part of Macbeth's mental breakdown: he is busy composing metaphors for sleep as an escape from the reality in which he finds himself. His mind is obviously deranged.

late stages of this scene. The knocking at the gate of the castle comes from the noblemen Lennox and Macduff, who have traveled here to meet the king. After we have entered the demonic world of the murders, the knocking suddenly brings us back to the outside world, sealing off the Macbeths in their world of demonic evil. The knocking also adds to the suspense of the moment, raising the possibility that the Macbeths will be caught in the act.

For Reflection or Discussion

First, it is important to work out in detail the ways in which Macbeth and Lady Macbeth are foils to each other in this scene. Second, this is a classic scene for the portrayal of the dynamics of guilt; how does Macbeth become a case study in the psychological and spiritual effects of guilt? Additionally, how does Shakespeare infuse a sense that this act of murder is far more than simply a physical horror? At the end of the scene, Macbeth expresses a wish that the murder had not occurred; what conclusions do you draw from the fact that Macbeth commits an act that he deplores before, during, and after committing it?

ACT 2, SCENE 3

Plot Summary

Macbeth's castle, near daybreak on the night of the murder. In contrast to the interior psychological scene preceding, this scene focuses on external action as the murder is discovered amid a flurry of commotion.

The scene opens with the "drunken porter's

speech." In it, the gatekeeper of the castle is awakened from his drunken sleep by the repeated knocking at the gate, knocking that had made an appearance already at the end of the preceding scene. In a comic scene that gets our minds off the oppressiveness of the murder, the porter imagines that he is the gatekeeper of hell and that people are arriving from earth. In sequence, he imagines the following characters and their offenses: a farmer who hoarded his crops in a false expectation that the next crop would be poor, an unscrupulous Jesuit priest, and a cheating tailor.

When Lennox and Macduff finally enter the castle, some good natured banter gives way to observations about unnatural happenings the night before (see Lennox's speech that begins at approximately line 50). Commotion next erupts as the murder is discovered and announced. Alarum bells ring, people enter the common room, there are entrances and exits, and we listen to excited voices that convey diverse messages—of discovery, shock, deceit (the Macbeths), and fear. Lady Macbeth either faints or pretends to faint and has to be carried out of the room. In a scene that could decline into anticlimax, Shakespeare wisely introduces an infusion of external action to generate interest and suspense.

Before the murder is announced, Lennox lists the unnatural events that occurred during the night (lines 52–57). This passage makes complete sense if placed into the Renaissance framework of the great chain of being. In this picture of the world, disorder on human levels (individual, family, civil) is inevitably matched by disorder on the cosmic level. This was so ingrained in Shakespeare's audience that they would have been expecting the events listed by Lennox.

Commentary

The genre of the murder story explains this scene. In a murder story the murder is discovered amidst high drama, and attention quickly turns to an attempt to discover who committed the murder. If the murderer is present, that person's cleverness in carrying out a cover-up grabs our attention. An additional ingredient of a murder story

Macduff's statement regarding Duncan's murder that "most sacrilegious murder hath broke ope / The Lord's anointed temple" alludes to two different passages in the Bible—the king as the Lord's anointed (1 Sam. 24:6; 2 Sam. 1:14) and the individual as God's anointed temple (1 Cor. 3:16–17).

is that suspicion for the murder initially falls on the wrong person(s). This motif takes two forms in this scene. (1) Macbeth murders the guards, ostensibly because he was overcome by rage, thereby preventing them from establishing their innocence. (2) At the end of the scene, the frightened sons of Duncan flee from Scotland for their lives (Malcolm to England and Donalbain to Ireland), an action that will very shortly cast suspicion on them for allegedly masterminding their father's execution.

For Reflection or Discussion

How do your experiences with murder stories (whether fictional ones or television programs about actual murders) enter your experience of this scene? What Christian or biblical echoes keep alive our awareness that we are moving in a Christian world in this play?

ACT 2, SCENE 4

Plot Summary

We hear Ross say in regard to the events of the past twelve hours, "'Gainst nature still." "Nature" here means the great chain of being. The unnatural happenings that are rehearsed in the opening lines of the scene are external signs and repercussions of the disorder that has engulfed the civil realm with the murder of the king.

Outside Macbeth's castle on the morning after the king's murder. This is a scene of closure, drawing a boundary around the murder, so we can move to its consequences in the next scene. In this low-voltage scene we listen to three people (Ross, an "old man," and Macduff) discuss the fallout from the king's murder. It is a "person on the street" scene, as well as a "morning after" scene. We listen to public responses to the unnatural events surrounding the murder, to the "official" version of who committed the murder (the drunken guards), and to news of the flight of Duncan's sons ("which puts upon them / Suspicion of the deed").

Commentary

It is important to start paying attention to Macduff from this point on, inasmuch as he is the person who will reestablish order at the end of the play. Already in the preceding scene when Macbeth announced that he had killed the guards, Macduff impaled him with the challenging question, "Wherefore did you so?" At the end of this scene, Macduff refuses to go to Scone to attend the coronation of Macbeth, symbolic of his refusal to accept the kingship of Macbeth. Furthermore, he utters an ironic or sarcastic statement about "old robes [sitting] easier than our new," thereby reinforcing the image pattern of ill-fitting garments that signals that Macbeth is not entitled to fill the role he has usurped.

"God's benison [blessing] go with you," the old man says to Macduff and Ross as they depart at the end of the scene. It is impossible to overstate the abundance of data that Shakespeare has put into this play (as well as other plays) to show that the characters in the world of the play accept Christian premises and utter Christian sentiments.

For Reflection or Discussion

All stories (especially those told by means of drama) are built on a principle of back-and-forth rhythm. After scenes of high tension and an abundance of external action, this one seems like a lull in the action. How do you respond to it? What conclusions can you reach about why Shakespeare thought it essential to his design?

ACT 3, SCENE 1

Plot Summary

Macbeth's royal palace at Forres, sometime after his coronation. Before we turn to scene 1, it is appropriate to take stock of the progress of the play up to this point. First, Macbeth was tempted by his own ambition and by certain external forces (his rising political fortunes, the witches' prophecy that he would be king, a pushy wife) to usurp the throne. The rising action of the plot consisted of the conflict between Macbeth's ambition for power and its deterrents. Before the murder, the chief obstacle was Macbeth's moral conscience. During the murder, Macbeth's inner antagonist was his psychological inadequacy to perform a murder. In this scene, Macbeth's ambition has a new foe—his feeling of insecurity now that he is king, especially in light of the witches' prophecy that Banquo would produce a line of kings.

As scene 1 of act 3 opens, some time has elapsed since Macbeth's coronation. Yet because we did not see the coronation, it is hard for us to picture Macbeth as king. Shakespeare's scanting him royal ceremonies is a way of suggesting that he is not entitled to them. The scene opens with a brief soliloquy in which Banquo expresses a suspicion that Macbeth has "played most foully" for the crown. He reflects further that if the witches' prophecies have thus come true for Macbeth, their prophecies that he himself would be the father of kings might come true also.

Apparently Macbeth has been thinking the same thing, for when he now enters the scene it becomes obvious that he is in the process of plotting the murder of Banquo and his son Fleance. Banquo is conveniently present at Macbeth's palace to be honored at the evening's dinner. But with time to kill before the end of the day, Banquo will naturally be busy with daytime activities. Macbeth

Another biblical subtext emerges in this scene. Macbeth becomes a latter-day King Saul, insecure in his kingship and paranoid about a suspected rival to his kingship (David in the case of Saul, Banquo in connection with Macbeth).

is murderously curious about exactly *how* Banquo plans to spend the afternoon.

Amidst small talk between Macbeth and Banquo on that subject, Macbeth asks three interspersed and highly charged questions designed to yield the information Macbeth needs to execute a murder. The three questions are these: "Ride you this afternoon?" "Is't far you ride?" "Goes Fleance with you?" This is an increasingly sinister sequence of questions, and Macbeth's mind is working very fast to process the information that he receives from Banquo. After Banquo exits the scene, Macbeth consults with hired murderers to execute Banquo and Fleance as they are out riding.

Commentary

The mainspring of the action in this scene is laid out in Macbeth's soliloquy in which he expresses his fears regarding Banquo. The subject of Macbeth's meditation is the insecurity he feels in his present role. He has become a clinical case of paranoia, always fearful of the "one" thing that stands in the way of his security. On this occasion "there is none but he [Banquo] / Whose being I do fear." But Macbeth is wrong when he says that this is the only thing he fears. His fears will continue to multiply. What he really wants is what he cannot have—the inner feeling of being king by right. Shakespeare has given us a case study in the psychology of guilt.

We can apply modern notions of psychology to Shakespeare's characters. In fact, psychologists are often captivated by how much Shakespeare knew about human psychology. In Shakespeare's day, however, psychology was very rudimentary,

The second half of the scene is devoted to Macbeth's extended negotiations with two hired murderers. Elsewhere in Shakespeare hired killers are dispatched with only a word or two. This long scene destroys any possible impression of casualness. Like the murder of Duncan, this act is fully premeditated.

so we need to credit Shakespeare with insights into human experience beyond the psychological theories of his day. In the Renaissance, psychology consisted primarily of "faculty psychology" that divided the human psyche into the faculties of reason, passion, will, and "fancy" (imagination, or our image-making capacity).

The scene ends with yet another reference to the Christian doctrine of heaven and hell, as the murder-plotting Macbeth says that Banquo's soul, "if it find heaven, must find it out to-night."

Even more importantly, the Renaissance conceived of psychology primarily in moral terms. In such a view, Macbeth's psychological aberrations are not only disorders of the mind and emotions but also of the soul. An important aspect of this is that at this point in the action the outside world does not yet know that Macbeth committed the murder. This means that Shakespeare is portraying the *self*-destructive effects of evil and guilt. At every point in Shakespeare's plays, we need to be aware that as a Renaissance author Shakespeare is concerned with people's total nature—physical, mental, emotional, moral, and spiritual.

For Reflection or Discussion

One avenue of exploration is to analyze the psychology at work in Macbeth in this scene. Another avenue is to observe Shakespeare's portrayal of moral decay in the life of a criminal; what are the evidences of that decline?

ACT 3, SCENE 2

Plot Summary

Macbeth's palace. This is the third of the great scenes dominated by the dynamics of guilt (the earlier ones being the dagger scene and the murder scene). The Macbeths are alone and bare their inner feelings to each other. It is a packed scene that yields a lot as we look closely at it.

The primary focus of the scene is the mutual insecurity and misery that the Macbeths experience. Since they are not yet suspected of the murder, it is obvious that Shakespeare's design is to portray the self-destructiveness of evil for the person who does it. As we listen to the exchange between husband and wife, we are led to feel the degree to which the Macbeths have failed to secure what they thought a crime would give them.

Commentary

The main point of this scene is a moral one: to commit evil without repenting of it is to destroy one's soul and life. It is not the outside world that is bringing the Macbeths to account; they are their own worst enemies and the agents of their own judgment, as they experience punishment for their crime before their crime is publicly exposed. Their misery is so deep that both of them express a death wish.

The audience sees what is happening, but the Macbeths do not: the focus of their discussion is not their guilt but their insecurity. Furthermore, in the murder scene Lady Macbeth had expressed the dismissive sentiment that "a little water clears of this deed." In this scene she continues in the same vein: "What's done is done" (line 12). She will come to change her mind later.

For Reflection or Discussion

This scene lends itself to both psychological and moral reflection. What are the effects of guilt on

Death as a release from burdensome reality or terrible suffering is an archetypal motif that has recurred throughout literature and life. In the Old Testament, the suffering Job expresses a sentiment not unlike Macbeth's portrayal of the deceased Duncan as being beyond the reach of earthly misfortune: "There the wicked cease from troubling, / and there the weary are at rest. / There the prisoners are at ease together; / they hear not the voice of the taskmaster" (Job 3:17–18).

To heighten the shock of the cruelty expressed in Macbeth's plans for further murder, Shakespeare fills the scene with terms of mutual tenderness between husband and wife, as Macbeth calls his wife by such terms of endearment as "love," "dear wife," "dearest chuck." A life of crime has drawn the couple closer together.

the mind and soul, not only in this scene but in our observations of life and our own experiences? When we scrutinize Macbeth and Lady Macbeth in this scene, they express a combination of insight and ignorance; at what moments do we see one of these and at what moments the other?

ACT 3, SCENE 3

Plot Summary

In the earlier scene where Macbeth had hired murderers, two murderers were present. In this murder scene, there are three murderers. Scholars have gone wild with speculation about the discrepancy. Probably the best explanation is that Macbeth, like any tyrant, cannot trust his underlings but must spy even on them.

A park near Macbeth's royal palace. Macbeth is absent from this scene. It is given over to the three hired murderers, who assault Banquo and his son Fleance as they are out riding. The murderers succeed in killing Banquo, but Fleance escapes.

Commentary

This brief scene exists solely to advance the plot. The murder of Banquo and escape of Fleance will both feed into the banquet scene that immediately follows. Macbeth's problems continue to multiply. The more evil Macbeth perpetrates, the more trouble he brings upon himself.

For Reflection or Discussion

This brief scene falls into a familiar narrative genre known as a scene of violence. It would be easy to dismiss this brief scene as not important enough to subject to analysis, but we need to operate on the premise that everything that a great writer puts into a literary work is important to the overall design. What does this scene of violence contribute to your experience and understanding of *Macbeth*?

ACT 3, SCENE 4

Plot Summary

The banqueting room of Macbeth's palace. Shakespeare's plays are so famous that many of the individual scenes are well known by the names scholars have pinned on them. This scene is obviously "the banquet scene" of *Macbeth*. It is also a ghost scene. The setting for this scene, the fourth scene governed by the dynamics of guilt, is the banquet hall in Macbeth's royal palace.

The multiple appearances of the ghost in this scene produce high drama. The rest of the characters look on in shocked amazement as Macbeth shouts at a ghost that is invisible to them with such outbursts as, "Thou canst not say I did it. Never shake / Thy gory locks at me." Something like the following will also disrupt a dinner party: "Avaunt, and quit my sight! Let the earth hide thee! / Thy bones are marrowless, thy blood is cold."

By contrast, the behavior of Lady Macbeth in this scene is very self-assured. Although she will undergo a mental breakdown shortly, she is still in control in this scene, reminiscent of her mastery of the situation in the murder scene. She assures the party that her husband "is often thus." She manages to keep the lid on an explosive situation, dismissing the lords hastily, but with no secrets having been divulged.

With the guests dismissed, Macbeth and Lady Macbeth take stock of what has happened. As the scene moves toward its conclusion, Macbeth collapses even further. First he falls back on the self-delusion that just one person is his problem: "How say'st thou, that Macduff denies his person / At our great bidding?" Desperate, Macbeth decides, "I

The problem of evil rulers who are a disgrace to a nation has always been around. The earliest texts on the subject are the Old Testament historical chronicles; the most recent ones are the daily news reports from around the world. To prompt your reflection on why this is the human predicament, you might conduct a Bible word search on the computer or in a topical Bible or concordance to find Bible verses that combine the words *heart* and *evil*. If you lack resources or time, have a look at these verses: Genesis 8:21; 2 Chronicles 12:14; Job 15:35; Proverbs 6:18; Matthew 15:19 (Mark 7:21 is the parallel verse); Luke 6:45. For a summary statement, see Jeremiah 17:9.

Macbeth's statement that "blood will have blood" is an allusion to one of the essential moral principles of the Bible, as stated definitively by God when laying down the ground rules for human life to Noah after the flood: "Whoever sheds the blood of man, by man shall his blood be shed" (Gen. 9:6).

While the allusion to Genesis 9:6 refers specifically to the sin of murder, the broader principle is that a person reaps what he or she sows. You can profitably look up some or all of the following biblical proverbs on sowing and reaping, and then reflect on your own experiences and observations of the principle in real life: Job 4:8; Proverbs 22:8; Hosea 8:7; 10:12; Galatians 6:7–8.

will to-morrow / (And betimes I will) to the weird sisters." Macbeth also vows to do terrible things. Instead of being deterred by the failure of his crimes to date, he plans to do still more criminal acts. Hand imagery reappears in the announcement, "Strange things I have in head, that will to hand" (line 139). The scene ends with the ominous one-liner, "We are yet but young in deed."

Commentary

We need to assemble information about what Shakespeare's society believed in regard to ghosts. Multiple theories existed. The ones that apply to this scene are four in number. (1) Ghosts are not a fiction of the imagination; they really exist in our world. (2) Sometimes, however, ghosts are hallucinations or tricks of the mind, visited upon people suffering from a particular kind of mental stress. In this play, the stress is obviously Macbeth's guilt. Although we are not intended to regard Banquo's ghost as having no objective existence in the world of the play, the fact that only Macbeth sees the ghost shows that Shakespeare drew upon *part* of the view that regarded ghosts as projections of people under stress. (3) Ghosts are supernatural portents (signs) of an impending and dreadful event; in this case the ghost both foreshadows and helps to bring about the further mental collapse and physical defeat of Macbeth. (4) Ghosts are spirits of the dead returned to earth to perform a deed left undone in life, including the exacting of revenge. The return of such a spirit is in effect a haunting, designed to get even with a murderer (for example) and if possible bring the murderer to justice. All of these theories explain the ghost of Banquo as a character in this scene.

Macbeth's psychology is central to the scene.

His self-delusion is evident in his conviction that just one person is always responsible for his fears and insecurity. When Macbeth says, "Then comes my fit again. I had else been perfect," he is wrong. His real foe is his guilt; this is the enemy he cannot conquer. The deepest meaning of the scene is Macbeth's festering conscience and guilt-haunted psyche. Macbeth sees the ghost because the ghost is a revenge ghost whose visit is designed for the person who killed Banquo.

When the Macbeths are alone at the end of the scene, they exchange speeches charged with moral insight. Two of the memorable statements by Macbeth express a universal insight into the moral principle of moral retribution for evil. In the first of these speeches, Macbeth observes that murdered people, instead of remaining dead, "rise again." Even more provocatively, "It will have blood, they say: blood will have blood." Lady Macbeth also expresses a thematic statement that sums up much of the meaning of a play devoted to the principle of the importance of order in the individual and society: "You [speaking to Macbeth] have displaced the mirth, broke the good meeting / With most admired disorder." All three speeches gesture toward the moral theme of justice and retribution.

This play gives us one gripping scene after another. Alfred Harbage comments, "A great wonder of this play is the way its hell-bound protagonists never relinquish their sway over our sympathetic imaginations. They struggle and suffer, and their language retains as points of reference the hopes, fears, and moral . . . perceptions of common humanity."

For Reflection or Discussion

Here is a scene that gives us a lot with which to work. First we can analyze what aspects of the

Shakespeare continues to model Macbeth on the Old Testament figure of King Saul. Like Saul, Macbeth is a king with a diseased mind. He is paranoid about supposed rivalry to his throne. He vows to consult witches. He is unable to sleep (as indicated by Lady Macbeth's observation, "You lack the season of all natures, sleep").

scene constitute good story material, asking, What is there about the action that draws me in and arouses my attention? What feelings are evoked within me? Then we can analyze the psychology at work in Macbeth. What insight does Shakespeare give us into the real-life phenomenon of powerful people performing feats of evil that seem without limit? How does this scene confirm the scholarly commonplace that although Shakespeare took the plot for this play from Holinshed's *Chronicles* of Scottish and English history, we move not so much in a world of English political history as in an Old Testament world in which the moral evil of a ruler contaminates a whole nation?

ACT 3, SCENE 5

Plot Summary

A heath. After the intense human interest of the banquet scene, this brief witch scene returns us to the supernatural backdrop for this story of evil. On a sinister heath, Hecate chides the three witches for "traffic[ing] with Macbeth" without her guidance. Then she instructs them to prepare their magic gear, so that when Macbeth comes to consult them they can entice Macbeth to his ruin with artificial demons distilled by Hecate from drops of the moon. The details of the plan are hazy, but the essence of the plan is to draw Macbeth "on to his confusion" by instilling a false security ("And you all know security / Is mortals' chiefest enemy").

Commentary

Shakespeare scholars generally do not like the scene and claim that it was not composed by

Hecate, from classical mythology, had multiple roles and powers. As Zeus's loyal daughter, she was given power over sky, earth, and sea. She was also goddess of the underworld, of the moon, and of sorcery and magic. Additionally, she was patroness of witches and helped them brew their potions. For us, the deities of classical mythology are purely fictitious, but that does not make them insignificant. We should regard them as *metaphors* of various aspects of reality.

Shakespeare. The main function of the scene is to return us to the world of supernatural evil that produced such impact on our imaginations early in the play. The discussion that we overhear among the witches foreshadows subsequent scenes.

For Reflection or Discussion

What feelings does a scene of supernatural evil like this evoke? What does the scene contribute to the play?

ACT 3, SCENE 6

Plot Summary

An unidentified place in Scotland. Lennox and a lord bring us up to date on developments in the broader world. Their speeches will make sense to us if we understand that they know that Macbeth is a murderer and usurper. The words of Lennox, for example, are full of second meanings and verbal irony (saying one thing and meaning the opposite). "The gracious Duncan / Was pitied of Macbeth," he says skeptically, adding, "Marry, he was dead." "Men must not walk too late," he says about Banquo, in implicit understanding that Macbeth is the one who orchestrated his murder in the dark. "How it did grieve Macbeth!" exclaims Lennox with mock awe.

The lord responds by telling us for the first time that Malcolm, rightful heir to Duncan's throne, has been living at the court of the king of England. We also learn that Macduff has gone there as well to enlist military aid in mounting an attack on Macbeth.

Religious terminology is woven into this scene designed to paint a positive picture of the English court and the forces that are beginning to converge to oppose Macbeth. Edward, king of England, is called "pious Edward." The military forces that are gathering will succeed "with Him [God] above / To ratify the work." Lennox expresses the wish that "some holy angel" might bring a message to the court of England. The lord concludes the scene with the sentiment, "I'll send my prayers with him." As is often the case with Shakespeare, in this play we are never allowed to lose sight of the fact that we are moving in a world that assumes the reality of the Christian faith.

Commentary

This may seem like a low-voltage scene, but it is the turning point (not to be confused with the climax) of the well-made plot of this play. Here are the phases up to this point: exposition (background to the story), inciting moment (the witches' prophecy), rising action (the triumph of Macbeth's ambition over his conscience, accompanied by his career in violence). The turning point of a plot is the point from which, especially at the end of the story, we can see how the conflict will eventually be resolved, even though we do not know the path that will takes us there. In this scene we hear for the first time about an organized resistance to Macbeth. The clock has begun to tick in the process that will bring Macbeth to justice. A counter-movement has begun.

For Reflection or Discussion

What aspects of the dialogue between Lennox and a nameless lord instill a new note of relief from the relentless power of evil that has dominated the action up to this point? Although we do not yet know the exact path by which we will arrive at the final destination of the story line, we know what the arrival will be; what is the destination that we infer from this scene?

ACT 4, SCENE 1

Plot Summary

A cave. As Macbeth's guilt and insecurity continue to torment him, he pays a return visit to the witches. Before he arrives, we are treated to one of the most celebrated witch scenes in Shakespeare's plays. The three witches rehearse a "grocery list" of repulsive ingredients for their evil brew. The function of the early part of the scene is atmospheric, as well as to perpetuate the characterization of the witches as grotesque and unnatural hags.

When Macbeth enters the scene, he conjures the witches. He receives two things from them—a pageant of "apparitions" (phantoms of people) who pass before him, and a series of three ambiguous or riddling prophecies, each of which is phrased in such a way as to conceal a hidden meaning. The three prophecies are these: (1) "beware Macduff"; (2) "none of woman born / Shall harm Macbeth"; (3) "Macbeth shall never vanquished be until / Great Birnam Wood to high Dunsinane Hill / Shall come against him."

In his curiosity, Macbeth wants to know one more thing: "Shall Banquo's issue [offspring] ever / Reign in this kingdom?" The witches at first refuse to answer but then arrange for Macbeth to see the future by looking into a magic glass. Macbeth sees a line of kings descended from Banquo.

The witches vanish as Lennox appears with the announcement that Macduff has fled to England. Macbeth responds with a soliloquy in which he vows that "From this moment / The very firstlings of my heart shall be / The firstlings of my hand." This is tacit admission that he had intended to kill Macduff, only to be frustrated in that intention by Macduff's escape. So Macbeth vows to attack Macduff's castle and kill his family.

With this scene we begin the phase of the well-made plot known as "further complication." With the turning point behind us, the action now turns to the story of Macbeth's struggle against external forces of retribution. This balances the rising action phase of the plot, which had consisted of Macbeth's struggle against *internal* obstacles (conscience, guilt, insecurity).

Commentary

Macbeth is famous for its evocation of atmosphere, and the function of the opening moments of this scene is to contribute to the atmosphere of demonic evil and foreboding. It is a principle of storytelling that the settings in a story are a fit "container" for the actions and agents that exist within them. In fact, we can ordinarily predict the quality of the events and characters that are about to occur. What is about to occur here is a temptation scene in which Macbeth receives information that pushes him onward in his career in evil. Of course it is Macbeth's twisted interpretation of each prophecy that transforms it into a temptation to proceed on his evil path, so it is important to analyze each one individually.

First, an apparition of an armed head represents Macduff, and the accompanying message is, "Beware Macduff." Macbeth is reassured to learn that his suspicions of his assumed antagonist are confirmed; he can handle *this*, he thinks. Second, the apparition of a bloody child (also representing Macduff) is accompanied by the prediction that "none of woman born / Shall harm Macbeth." Macbeth wrongly thinks that this means he is immune from death at the hand of Macduff, since it turns out that Macduff was brought into the world by caesarian birth and therefore not exactly born in the usual way. The third apparition is a child crowned (symbolizing Malcolm), with a tree in his hand. The accompanying prophecy is that Macbeth will never be vanquished "until / Great Birnam Wood to high Dunsinane Hill / Shall come against him." Macbeth is again lulled into a false security because he theorizes that a forest cannot move.

There is much to remind us here of Macbeth's first encounter with the witches. In that earlier encounter, the witches had uttered three prophecies that became a temptation for Macbeth to kill

Birnam Wood and Dunsinane Hill are places in Scotland. Dunsinane is a hill on which Macbeth's castle stands at this point in the action, and where he is finally defeated. Birnam is a forest-covered hill located twelve miles from Dunsinane Hill.

A biblical subtext underlies Shakespeare's handling of this scene. Macbeth here becomes a latter-day King Saul—a doomed and paranoid king near the point of death consulting a witch because he is fearful of his future. 1 Samuel 28 makes a good parallel text for this scene.

the king. In this second meeting with the witches, Macbeth receives another trio of prophecies that propels him into a false sense of immunity from retribution as he undertakes a new cycle of evil.

For Reflection or Discussion

The opening conversation among the witches is an example of the grotesque imagination—the deliberate evocation of abnormal sensations as a way of awakening repulsion; what are the means by which Shakespeare arouses our sense of repulsion toward the unnatural? How do the speeches contribute toward the portrayal of evil in this play? When the scene shifts to Macbeth, it is possible (as always) to subject Macbeth to psychological analysis: how does Shakespeare take us inside the twisted mind of a criminal who increasingly loses contact with reality?

ACT 4, SCENE 2

Plot Summary

Macduff's castle at Fife. As the scene opens, Macduff's wife complains to her kinsman Ross about her husband's trip to England. Ross consoles her by arguing that Macduff's motives are good. After Ross leaves, Macduff's wife and her son engage in whimsical conversation about the absence of the head of the household. Shakespeare's strategy here is to evoke an idealized picture of normal civilized life, just before it is annihilated in an act of barbarism.

The banter between mother and son is the ironic "false calm" before the storm, a favorite

This scene is unpleasant to watch in performance, and the portrayal of Macduff's precocious-sounding son has always seemed a little implausible. The scene can be salvaged in our thinking if we examine the function that it serves in the play as a whole.

strategy of storytellers. A messenger arrives to urge Macduff's wife to flee with her children, but the warning comes too late. Murderers arrive, inquire where Macduff is, kill the boy, and pursue the wife offstage as she cries, "Murder!"

There may be a biblical subtext at work in this scene. Macbeth's murderers enter a home and kill an innocent family, including a young child. The archetype at work is known as "the murder of the innocents," a subject particularly common in medieval and Renaissance paintings. The original story of the murder of the innocents is part of the nativity story as told in Matthew 2:16–18.

Commentary

This scene of horror is extraneous to the main plot, but it serves the purpose of further characterizing Macbeth as a hardened criminal who has killed his conscience through long habit of sin. One of the unifying motifs in *Macbeth* is the criminal's abandonment of himself to a life of crime. Such abandonment to evil is one of the terrors of life, and it is as up-to-date as the latest television news cast.

The violence of this scene runs the risk of seeming gratuitous (thrown in for the sake of sensational effect). But several things make it warranted. One of the things that *Macbeth* does is give shape to our terrors; it is truthful to a certain side of life. Life in our world is often violent. One of the purposes of literature is to make us confront life instead of running away from it. This scene does so.

For Reflection or Discussion

How are dramatic irony and foreshadowing present in the scene? How do you assimilate and/or interpret the portrayal of violence in the scene?

ACT 4, SCENE 3

Plot Summary

The English court. This extended scene is long on talk and short on action. The main content is a conversation that takes place between Malcolm and Macduff in the court of the English king. We need to remember that Malcolm had fled to the English court for asylum after his father was killed. Furthermore, Malcolm had been announced by King Duncan to be his heir to the throne.

Additional background information for the scene is as follows: Macduff is the military power broker who will defeat Macbeth and pave the way for Malcolm's ascent to the throne. Malcolm, though, feels a need to prove to himself the integrity of this strong man, so he stages a mock accusation of himself to ascertain Macduff's response. His need to feel out the integrity of his prospective ally suggests the degree to which mistrust has become a way of life in the chaotic political world of Scotland.

The conversation opens with Macduff's bewailing of the chaos that has befallen Scotland with the rule of Macbeth. "Each new morn / New widows howl, new orphans cry," says Macduff in his litany of misfortune. After Macduff and Malcolm have duly lamented the sad state of affairs in their native country, Malcolm springs a surprise on both Macduff and us by staging a mock accusation of himself. He paints a picture of himself as a worse tyrant than Macbeth and as a morally corrupt person. In fact, he eventually claims that he lacks all of "the king-becoming graces," which he proceeds to list. Malcolm claims that he has "no relish of them."

Malcolm's self-accusation had been stage-managed to evoke a response from Macduff. It does just that: Macduff erupts in horror, concluding that Malcolm is not fit to govern or even to live. He concludes his outburst by addressing his own heart

With this scene we need remind ourselves that *Macbeth* is a political play that raises the question of good and bad rule. The conversation about the effects of tyrannical rule touches upon a recurrent problem of human society. As far back as Plato, thinking people have agonized over the difficulty of finding good rulers, and especially rulers who are not corrupted by power.

and declaring, "Thy hope ends here." Malcolm is greatly relieved. Macduff's revulsion toward misrule and moral corruption, claims Malcolm, has "reconciled my thoughts / To thy good truth and honor" (lines 116–17). With his fears now silenced, Malcolm further puts himself under the protection of Macduff as military strong man. Another Scottish nobleman, Siward, is already poised to invade Scotland with an army of ten thousand soldiers.

When the exchange between Macduff and Malcolm ends, our attention is directed to the English King Edward, the norm for a good king who functions as a foil to the villainous Macbeth. Edward does not actually enter the story, but a doctor and Malcolm both utter speeches that build up in our imaginations the legend of the healing powers of the saintly king. Suddenly we are in a totally different world from the world of physical and moral chaos represented by Macbeth's Scotland. In fact, here we find the reverse situation: instead of a king who brings disease to a society, King Edward possesses miraculous powers of healing—a "healing benediction"—as well as "a heavenly gift of prophecy" (lines 156–57).

Ross, a nobleman of Scotland, arrives on the scene to confirm the sad state of affairs in Scotland. The "poor country," he says, "cannot / Be called our mother but our grave" (line 166). Each minute brings a new grief. After obvious reluctance to deliver the message, Ross informs Macduff that his castle has been surprised and his family slaughtered by Macbeth's men. The question of how Macduff will respond to such devastating news lends some suspense to a scene that has been largely devoid of intensity. As the scene ends, spurred on by Malcolm, Macduff accepts the

A popular literary genre of Shakespeare's day was known as "the mirror for magistrates." Such literature held a mirror up to rulers in which they could see their own virtues and vices and respond appropriately. A good approach to *Macbeth* is to view it as belonging to this genre and to analyze what instruction a ruler might derive from assimilating this play. Then we can legitimately think of examples from the Bible that belong to the genre of the mirror for magistrates.

slaughter of his family as a "whetstone" to sharpen his sword to exact justice from Macbeth. The concluding line of the scene sums up this resolve: "The night is long that never finds the day."

Commentary

This scene is a pause in the action, a lull between flurries of violence. What precedes and follows is so intense and emotionally taxing as to warrant an interlude. The main function of this long scene is to establish the integrity of Malcolm and Macduff, the two leaders who will eventually set matters right in Scotland and assume power after they have disposed of the villainous Macbeth.

Malcolm's list of "king-becoming graces," by which he means "virtues that characterize an ideal king," serves as a foil to the breakdown of morality that we have observed in the play thus far. Suddenly we are given a moral norm or standard that highlights what we have witnessed the breakdown of. This brief list of moral virtues rings out almost like the famous "fruit of the Spirit" passage in Galatians 5:22–23.

There are additional spiritual implications in this scene as well. The brief account of the English king's supernatural powers, part of a grand foil to Macbeth's linkage with supernatural powers of evil, is based on Christian belief (universally held in English society in Shakespeare's day) that the spirit world is comprised of both good and evil agents. We hear so much about the demonic supernatural in this play that this passage suddenly opens up a view of *God's* spiritual power. The vocabulary itself is spiritually charged, with words such as *sanctity, miraculous work, holy prayers, healing benediction, heavenly gift, blessings,* and *full of grace.*

Shakespeare is legendary for packing his words with multiple meanings. A good example is Macduff's statement when he has heard of Macbeth's murder of his family and has just been told by Malcolm to "be comforted" and resolve to exact a "great revenge." Macduff's one-liner is, "He has no children." Three plausible interpretations have been suggested: (a) if Malcolm had children of his own, he would know better than to offer revenge as an adequate comfort; (b) because Macbeth has no children, Macduff cannot exact revenge in kind; (c) if Macbeth had children of his own, he would never have slaughtered Macduff's children.

When Malcolm tells Macduff to "dispute it like a man" (line 220), he means, "Resist or struggle against your grief with courage."

The specific disease over which King Edward was reputed by legend to have power is simply called "the evil." We know from other sources that this "king's evil," as it was called, was scrofula, an enlargement and deterioration of the lymphatic glands, especially of the neck. Tellingly, the entry "scrofulous" in the dictionary carries as one of its definitions "morally corrupt; degenerate," again heightening the contrast between Edward (health-bringing) and Macbeth (morally diseased).

For Reflection or Discussion

Literature as a whole has a double subject: (1) the world that the human race longs for and aspires to create; (2) the real-life obstacles that get in the way of establishing that ideal world. In act 4, scene 2, we are reminded of the archetypal "bad place" that dominates *Macbeth* and are given a brief utopian vision of the archetypal "good place"; what things fill out the picture of those two imagined places? What real-life examples of these two worlds can you name? What Christian doctrines undergird the pessimistic assessment of political institutions that Shakespeare gives us in *Macbeth*? What view of the person emerges from this play's portrayal of power and rule?

ACT 5, SCENE 1

Plot Summary

Macbeth's castle. This is one of Shakespeare's great scenes—so famous that of course it bears its own name. It is known as "the sleepwalking scene." In it, Lady Macbeth walks about the castle by night, wringing her hands and uttering a soliloquy that is overheard by her maid and doctor.

The scene opens with a bit of setup: Lady Macbeth's maid ("gentlewoman") is understandably alarmed by her lady's practice of sleepwalking, and even more by what is revealed by the hand-washing ritual and the accompanying utterances of Lady Macbeth. So she has enlisted a doctor to watch the spectacle with her. On the third night of this stakeout, Lady Macbeth performs her ritual. The utterances of Lady Macbeth follow a stream-of-consciousness structure, following the random association of thoughts as they actually occur in a person's mind.

After wandering about, Lady Macbeth blows out her candle and returns to bed. The scene ends with the doctor's verdict on what he has observed. His response is charged with Christian insight: "More needs she the divine [the Christian minister] than the physician. / God, God forgive us all." The latter statement universalizes Lady Macbeth's sin and guilt as the universal human condition from which no one is exempt.

Commentary

The foregoing summary of the external action barely hints at what happens in this scene at the psychological and spiritual levels. The famous sleepwalking scene is governed by the dynamics of the self-destructiveness of evil and the debilitating effects of guilt.

Directors agree that the scene should not be played too strenuously. What we are supposed to notice is the change that has occurred in Lady Macbeth. She is now a broken woman, weak and ill. The last time she appeared on stage was in

In a play that has been filled with psychological portrayal of inner states of mind and soul, this scene may outrank all the others. In keeping with the realistic, clinical observation of a patient that goes on in the scene, the scene is written in prose rather than poetry.

It is nearly impossible to overpraise Shakespeare's ability to portray human psychology. Some of the best commentary on this scene comes from professional psychologists. Some psychiatrists report clients who have exhibited exactly the same actions that Lady Macbeth performs in this scene. The technical term for physical ailments that stem from psychological causes is *psychosomatic*.

the banquet scene, where she somehow managed to keep the lid on an explosive situation. She is now a virtual invalid, beset with physical and psychological collapse. Alfred Harbage writes regarding the scene, "Though there has been no intervening mention of change, we are not surprised by it; we have already surmised that her apparent ferocity was in a measure bravado, was sustained by an effort, that she was not a fiend by birth."

Two things govern the scene. One is the actions that Lady Macbeth performs. Sleepwalking is the main action, within which the others occur. While walking in her sleep, Lady Macbeth performs symbolic ritual actions. The chief one is the incessant wringing of hands to suggest washing them. Her walking and moving from her bedroom into the adjoining room may subtly suggest an urge to escape from inner torment. In regard to the hand motion, hand imagery has been a unifying image pattern in the play. Early in the play it represented the agent of the murder. But once the murder is perpetrated, the hand has mainly been a bloody hand, symbol of guilt and retribution.

In addition to her physical movement and hand washing, Lady Macbeth talks in her sleep. Lady Macbeth's speeches intermingle psychological insight and spiritual awareness. On the psychological level, two archetypes are present. One is sleeplessness as a symbol of unrelieved guilt. Another is the impulse of a criminal to relive the circumstances of a crime or even to return to the scene of the crime, an outworking of the impulse to confess the crime. In some of the lines, it is

Pilate's hand-washing routine is one of the biblical subtexts for this scene, but Psalm 32:1–4 is another. Part of that passage reads, "Blessed is the one whose transgression is forgiven. . . . For when I kept silent, . . . day and night your hand was heavy upon me: my strength was dried up as by the heat of summer."

obvious that Lady Macbeth is reliving the murders that she and her husband have perpetrated.

Other statements denote a level of spiritual reality beyond psychological reality. Her handwashing routine, accompanied by the statement, 'Yet here's a spot," expresses awareness of guilt stemming from sin and the need to be washed clean from it. The question, "Who would have thought the old man to have had so much blood in him?" calls attention to the principle of retribution for murder, along the lines of God's mandate in Genesis 9:6—"Whoever sheds the blood of man, by man shall his blood be shed." Thus as Lady Macbeth relives the murders, there arises from her subconscious and her conscience a reservoir of spiritual insight.

One of the key utterances by Lady Macbeth in this scene is the statement, "What's done cannot be undone." This needs to be contrasted to her comment in act 3, scene 2, that "what's done is done." There is a subtle difference in the statement here. In the earlier scene, Lady Macbeth's statement was dismissive of the idea that there could be any long-term effect from the murder. The statement in the sleepwalking scene implies a wish that the murder *could* be undone.

In this scene Shakespeare yet again builds upon a biblical subtext. Obviously the futile attempt to wash blood from the hands is a biblical allusion to the actions of Pilate on the morning of Christ's crucifixion. Lady Macbeth becomes a latter-day Pilate, futilely washing her hands in a wished-for innocence. Matthew 27:24 is the baseline on which Shakespeare works.

A main function of this scene is to bring the characterization of Lady Macbeth to its conclu-

When the doctor says that Lady Macbeth needs "the divine" more than "the physician," he means that she needs the Christian minister or pastor (called a "divine" in Shakespeare's day) rather than a medical doctor. Her root ailment, of which her physical aberrations are mere symptoms, is sin and guilt, and the remedy is not psychological therapy but forgiveness of sin by God, the message above all others that a minister of the gospel proclaims.

Fiction boasts some other notable examples of the motif of a criminal returning to the scene of a crime and/or reliving a scene of horror in one's sleep. Examples include Edgar Allan Poe's short story *The Tell Tale Heart* and Russian author Fyodor Dostoyevsky's novel *Crime and Punishment*.

sion. She has been a thoroughly developing character, ending virtually at the opposite end of the continuum from where she began. In the murder scene, she had casually said, "A little water clears us of this deed. / How easy is it then!" Now she claims that "all the perfumes of Arabia will not sweeten this little hand." In view of Lady Macbeth's aggressiveness in the first half of the play, the reference to "this little hand" catches us by surprise and is a visual reminder that Lady Macbeth is small of stature and frail of constitution.

For Reflection or Discussion

As you work your way through the scene, where do you see psychological experience portrayed, and where do you see spiritual insight expressed? Another way of getting at this is to ascertain in which lines Lady Macbeth is either (a) revisiting the scene of the crime, confessing the crime, or reliving the murders of Duncan, Banquo, and Macduff's family, and (b) extracting the spiritual implications of the murders that she and her husband have committed. The scene is memorable for its catchy one-liners; what deeper meanings do you see in each of the following statements?

1) "Yet here's a spot."
2) "Hell is murky."
3) "Yet who would have thought the old man to have had so much blood in him?'"
4) "What, will these hands ne'er be clean?"
5) "Here's the smell of the blood still."
6) "More needs she the divine than the physician."

ACT 5, SCENE 2

Plot Summary

A field near Dunsinane. This brief scene tells us what we need to know about the preparations for the coming battle between the army from England and Macbeth's army. We need to remind ourselves that this phase of the plot concentrates on Macbeth's struggle against external agents of retribution, to balance the first half of the play, where the conflict was mainly an internal struggle between Macbeth's ambition and its inner foes.

We learn first that an English force has arrived in Scotland, led by Malcolm, his uncle Siward, and Macduff. Also present is the youthful son of Siward, along with "many unrough youths" who are about to undergo their initiation into warfare (an archetype of literature). Our interest is naturally piqued by mention of Birnam Wood and Dunsinane, since both sites had been mentioned in one of the witches' ambiguous prophecies.

Image patterns figure prominently in all of Shakespeare's great tragedies. The imagery of hands and ill-fitting garments appears in this scene.

We also learn that Macbeth is fortifying his castle at Dunsinane. He is pictured as doomed but defiant. A nobleman named Angus reminds us of two master images in the play when he comments that Macbeth now feels "his secret murders sticking on his hands," and his title hanging "loose about him, like a giant's robe / Upon a dwarfish thief." As the scene ends, the noblemen "march towards Birnam."

Commentary

In every play there are brief scenes known as "functional scenes" that are inserted to help explain major scenes that follow. Act 5, scene 2, is a functional scene. The play is now poised to move toward its climax, which will occur on the battlefield. Before we arrive there, we need a picture of battle preparations, and that is what we get in this scene.

If the scene thus looks forward to future action, it also looks backward. In view of the witches' prophecies involving Dunsinane and Birnam, our ears perk up when we hear those names mentioned in this scene.

For Reflection or Discussion

What echoes of earlier parts of the play appear in this scene? What elements created foreshadowing and suspense? What meanings are embodied in the imagery of hands and ill-fitting garments?

ACT 5, SCENE 3

Plot Summary

Macbeth's castle. The preceding scene was devoted to the converging forces arrayed against Macbeth, and now we are transported to the castle of Macbeth. Part of our attention flows to the plot, as we learn about Macbeth's fortification of his castle as he anticipates an attack.

Hovering over the entire scene is Macbeth's ill temper to everyone around him. He is a person out of control. Fueling his intolerable behavior is his ironic belief that he is invulnerable, as his last words in the scene highlight: "I will not be afraid of death and bane / Till Birnam Forest come to Dunsinane."

More profoundly, though, this scene is devoted to the character development of Macbeth. Spurred by the ambiguous or riddling prophecies of the witches, Macbeth now operates under a great delusion: he thinks himself immune from death. That is the import of his opening lines in this scene, where he dismisses reports about invading forces. In fact, like some other famous military leaders facing defeat, he isolates himself from the facts, commanding that no further reports be brought to him. In his opening speech, Macbeth cites the speeches of the witches to explain why reports cannot "taint [him] with fear."

Macbeth utters two famous soliloquies late in the play, and one of them occurs in this scene, beginning with the line, "My way of life / Is fall'n into the sear, the yellow leaf." Macbeth proceeds to list the human values that "should accompany old age" but to which he has relinquished a claim by his tyrannical behavior. Instead of the honor and loyalty that a person hopes to attain in old age, Macbeth has earned only curses and phony honor that his subordinates grudgingly give him because they are afraid to do otherwise.

Half of the scene is devoted to Macbeth the general, but then Shakespeare deftly shifts the focus to the domestic half of Macbeth's life. Thus we have an exchange between Macbeth the husband and his wife's doctor, as the doctor brings Macbeth up-to-date on his wife's worsening condition. In this exchange, too, Macbeth is dismissive. He says regarding his wife's illness, "Cure her of that! / Canst thou not minister to a mind diseased?" It is a naive "magic wand" approach, as out of touch with reality as Macbeth's dismissal of the alarms that are being sounded in regard to a coming military attack.

In literary tragedy, the tragic hero gradually becomes isolated from his society. In the latter stages of this play, Macbeth is mainly seen on stage with only one other character at a time. One of these characters is named Seyton, a pun on the word *Satan*. There is obvious irony and symbolic significance to Macbeth's being alone with Seyton = Satan.

Commentary

Shakespeare's strategy in act 5 is for the scenes to shuttle back and forth between the invading forces in the countryside and Macbeth in his castle. An important concern in the castle scenes is the continuing development of Macbeth. Here in scene 3, the moral and psychological collapse of Macbeth stands silhouetted before us.

The doomed Macbeth remains defiant to the end. At one point he says, "I'll fight till from my bones my flesh be hacked. / Give me my armor." If our sympathy for courage flows toward Macbeth at such a moment, it quickly ebbs when he responds to the doctor's account of Lady Macbeth's mental breakdown with the insensitive command, "Cure her of that! / Canst thou not minister to a mind diseased?" This is a moment of moral decline from Macbeth's earlier characterization. In the murder scene, Macbeth had been acutely aware of the moral guilt that attached to the murder he had committed, even expressing the fear that his hand would never again be clean. Now he reduces his wife's guilt to a mere disease, and he seems angry that the doctor cannot cure it. In contrast to the sentiment of the murder scene that his blood-stained hand will redden the entire ocean, he now tells the doctor to "cast / The water of my land" and "purge" his wife's disease.

It is a convention of literary tragedy that late in the action the tragic hero comes to a moment of tragic perception (also called tragic recognition)—an insight into what caused the tragic downfall. Ordinarily a speech of tragic recognition is the tragic hero's acknowledgment of the bad choice and flaw of character that led to the catastrophe. The speech in which the hero expresses this insight stands out as important and heightened. Macbeth never attains full tragic perception, but there are two memorable speeches late in the play that are a version of the tragic hero's moment of recognition.

The first occurs in this scene and consists of a soliloquy that begins with the statement, "My way of life / Is fall'n into the sear, the yellow leaf." It is a "taking stock" speech, as the moment of tragic

Macbeth claims that his life has fallen into "the sear, the yellow leaf." "Sear" means "dry and withered"; together the phrases assert that his life is in its autumn season, a season of decline and (in literature generally) a tragic archetype. Macbeth also says that he can expect only curses and "mouth-honor" from his subordinates. "Mouth-honor" means words of honor and respect that are spoken out of fear rather than genuinely felt.

perception always is. Macbeth lists the human experiences and relationships that he has forfeited by his life of crime. While Macbeth does not see that his own tragic choice is what has brought this deprivation upon him, his speech fulfills the function of the conventional moment of perception by showing that Macbeth is aware of what he has lost.

There is an element of paradox in the speech. Although Macbeth has become an unfeeling murderer, he is also capable of sensitivity into human values. Here, in memorable poetry, Macbeth is able to name the precious human values for which any person would long ("honor, love, obedience, troops of friends"), along with his awareness of his own status as the archetypal outcast. One commentator calls the words "sad and beautiful; this is truly the poetry of the soul in anguish" (Harbage).

For Reflection or Discussion

Two things require our pondering. One is the ongoing development of Macbeth's characterization in the play. In particular, we should explore his moral decline in this scene. Second, his speech of partial perception can be analyzed for its beautiful poetry and its commentary on the tragic action of the play as a whole.

ACT 5, SCENE 4

Plot Summary

The countryside near Birnam Wood. The camera now swings back to the countryside where the invading army continues its preparation for the climactic battle. The resistance force is mov-

The Elizabethan stage (the theater in Shakespeare's day) possessed some paradoxical qualities. Because of the outdoor setting of the theaters, coupled with frequent changes of scenes within the plays, there were very few stage props (elements of physical scenery on the stage). Yet costumes were elaborate. It is no wonder that battle scenes were an absolute favorite, with actors in bulky military garb and swords swaggering over the stage. Being a political play, *Macbeth* ends with the military spectacle that the original audiences loved.

ing in on Macbeth's castle. Most important of all is the strategy of every soldier cutting down a bough from a tree and holding it in front of him, thereby disguising the extent of the numbers of the approaching army.

Commentary

This is strictly a "plot scene," designed to build a sense of anticipation about the climactic battle. The voltage of the scene stems from the fact that the forest where the army is located is not just any forest. It is nothing less than "the Wood of Birnam." This triggers our memory that one of the witches' prophecies had been that "Macbeth shall never vanquished be until / Great Birnam Wood to high Dunsinane Hill / Shall come against him." Macbeth has all along interpreted this to mean that he is invulnerable, but we now see that Birnam Wood is coming to Macbeth's castle at Dunsinane.

ACT 5, SCENE 5

Plot Summary

Inside Macbeth's castle. This is a major scene because of two famous speeches by Macbeth. The context for those speeches is the impending battle. Macbeth begins the scene with defiance, commanding that banners be hung on his castle walls as a gesture of defiance toward the approaching enemy army. He asserts that his "castle's strength / Will laugh a siege to scorn." But things decline from there.

The next phase of action is occasioned by "a cry within of women," meaning that from within the castle comes the sound of wailing women. When Macbeth's servant Seyton leaves to discover the cause of the wailing, Macbeth utters a soliloquy in which he details how insensitive he has become to terror as a result of his criminal life. Seyton returns to announce that Lady Macbeth is dead (by suicide, we learn in a later scene). Macbeth responds by taking us even further into his inner soul, as he expresses his sentiment that life is meaningless, in a famous speech that begins "tomorrow, and tomorrow, and tomorrow."

Following these excursions into Macbeth's inner psychic world, our attention shifts back toward the external turmoil of the impending battle. A messenger arrives to announce that Birnam Wood is, in fact, moving toward Dunsinane. Macbeth responds by expressing doubt about the immunity that he had thought the witches' prophecy had conferred on him.

Commentary

The heart of this famous scene is two soliloquies in which Macbeth lays bare his inner state of mind and soul. It is important to our experience of both speeches to be fully aware that the speaker is a criminal at the end of his career in crime and evil. In keeping with the pattern of the gradual isolation of the tragic hero, we can note again that Macbeth's only companions on stage in this scene are, in sequence, the ominously named Seyton (= Satan) and a nameless messenger.

When Seyton leaves Macbeth for the purpose of checking on the wailing of the women within the castle, Macbeth utters a soliloquy in which he meditates on the effect of a life of crime and violence on his sensitivities. The keynote is that Mac-

Macbeth's famous "tomorrow and tomorrow" soliloquy is a mosaic or collage of biblical quotations. Reading some of the biblical passages in their context is a requirement of a full experience of Shakespeare's great creation in this soliloquy. Here are some starting suggestions. On the overall theme, Ecclesiastes 1:2. On the phrase "dusty death," Genesis 3:19; Job 10:1, 9; Psalm 22:15. On the phrase "brief candle," Job 18:5–6. On the image of "walking shadow," Job 8:9; 14:1–2; Psalms 102:11; 144:4; and Ecclesiastes 8:13. On life as a tale that is told, Psalm 90:8–9.

beth has "almost forgot the taste of fears" and that he has "supped full with horrors." He is so accustomed to fear and horror that he is now unmoved by them.

When Seyton returns from his research trip with the news, "The Queen, my lord, is dead," Macbeth responds with a one-liner that sends the critics into ecstasy: "She should have died hereafter." Three main interpretations exist: (1) she would have died sooner or later anyway (an expression of utter indifference); (2) she died prematurely (a neutral observation); (3) her death should have occurred later in life; she deserved a kinder death (a statement of regret). Perhaps the very ambiguity is important: Macbeth cannot find certainty.

Then follows the most famous speech in the play, which is also one of Shakespeare's most famous soliloquies. It begins "tomorrow, and tomorrow, and tomorrow." The keynote of the speech is that life is futile and meaningless. Macbeth here denies a basic premise of human life (perhaps *the* basic premise for living)—that life has meaning. It is important to keep in mind that a criminal is the one who is talking, and he is speaking at the end of his career as a criminal. The speech is certainly not Shakespeare's philosophy of life. It is a very poetic speech, and we should pause to note that Macbeth speaks with a poetic eloquence unsurpassed among Shakespearean characters. (This is one reason, among others, why we sympathize with Macbeth despite his criminal character).

Ending the scene with a return to the external battle is a stroke of genius on Shakespeare's part. *Macbeth* blends the inner world of the mind and soul with the external events that make that inner

It is rare that a writer would choose a criminal as his tragic hero, but Shakespeare made that move in *Macbeth*. Perhaps for this reason, the "tomorrow and tomorrow" soliloquy, placed where we are expecting the usual moment of tragic perception, only partly meets the requirements of that convention of tragedy. Certainly Macbeth is aware that something has gone wrong in his life, but the speech contains no insight into what Macbeth has done to cause the situation in which he finds himself. His speech falls short of expressing a sense of personal wrongdoing and sinfulness, though it expresses the degree to which he finds life meaningless.

We can give the moment of tragic perception a theological angle by saying that the tragic hero's conventional speech of recognition is a moment of confession for having done a sinful act. Macbeth does not make that confession. Psalm 51 is a good expression of what Macbeth should have done.

world possible. Playwrights cannot build a drama out of internal events only.

For Reflection or Discussion

In what ways does the scene contribute to our understanding of Macbeth and his development as a character? Additionally, the poetry of Macbeth's two soliloquies is marvelous and lends itself to explication. The two speeches are haunting in their verdict on life; in what ways do you resonate with the feelings that Macbeth expresses? In what ways does the "tomorrow and tomorrow" soliloquy measure up to the tragic convention of the hero's moment of recognition, and in what ways does it fall short of the usual moment of tragic perception?

ACT 5, SCENE 6

Plot Summary

A field outside Macbeth's castle. For anyone who likes brief scenes, this one ranks among the best! In yet another plot scene, we catch a glimpse of the invading army preparing for attack. Ten lines suffice to convey a sense of battle commotion and noise, as the invading army readies for attack.

Commentary

The Renaissance stage was virtually devoid of stage props, but noise was a common strategy. A scene like this would have consisted of three soldiers making a sudden appearance on the stage in full armor and shouting a few battle commands, with banging and trumpet sounds in the background as they exited. That would have been enough to generate a sense of battle excitement.

In a striking image, Macbeth begins the scene by evoking the scene of a bear baiting—a low form of entertainment in Shakespeare's day in which a bear would be tied to a stake and baited by dogs or men. Macbeth describes himself as "tied . . . to a stake. I cannot fly, / But bear-like I must fight the course." It is almost as though Shakespeare wrote the script for Hitler's final days at the end of the Second World War.

Macbeth encounters young Siward in battle and kills him. Then Macduff enters the fray, and we expect something *really* big to ensue. He exits for the moment, though, and we are left with random bits of battlefield commotion. Storytellers love to use delaying tactics that heighten our sense of anticipation for major events.

ACT 5, SCENE 7

Plot Summary

Another part of the battlefield. This scene (and the following one) gave Shakespeare's original audience the sword play that they loved. This is a typical battle scene, whether in epic literature or a political play like *Macbeth*. There are brandishing of weapons, single combats, speeches of boasting and defiance and challenge, falling bodies, shouts of exultation or defeat, and the sounding of alarms on drums or bells.

Commentary

The experiences of reading a play and seeing the play performed are very different. In reading *Macbeth*, the poetic passages are the most rewarding, while the action scenes are likely to drag. In performance, the poetic speeches are often too packed to yield their meanings and seem to fly right past us, whereas the action scenes come alive. That dynamic is fully operative in this brief scene of battlefield action. We must, however, keep the overall conceptual framework of the play in view: the battlefield action here at the end of the play is an outworking of a principle of judgment against evil.

For Reflection or Discussion

The "martial theme" (the portrayal of battlefield action, replete with the conventions listed above in the plot summary section) was the main subject matter for centuries for imaginative literature, starting especially with ancient epics. It is important for us as modern readers to engage in some introspection and decide how we personally respond to the portrayal of military action as literary subject matter.

ACT 5, SCENE 8

Plot Summary

Another part of the battlefield. Battle action now takes center stage, as the play becomes somewhat melodramatic. The climax of the play is the single combat between Macbeth and Macduff. Macbeth undergoes his ultimate moment of disillusionment when he incorrectly claims that he bears "a charmed life." What Macbeth means by that statement is that he is invulnerable because the witches had prophesied that "none of woman born / Shall harm Macbeth." But Macduff explains that he "was from his mother's womb / Untimely ripped," that is, born by cesarean operation. The climax comes with Macbeth's death at the sword point of Macduff.

But a climax is always followed by denouement—the tying up of loose ends. Here the denouement consists of (1) the announcement that the noble young Siward (son of Ross) died in battle, (2) Macduff's entering with Macbeth's head and announcing that "the time is free," (3) the soldiers' hailing Malcolm as king, and (4) Malcolm announcing the political arrangements for the immediate future.

Commentary

We can profitably begin by recalling the shape of the action according to the framework of the "well-made plot." The first half of the play follows the sequence of exposition—inciting moment (also called "inciting force")—rising action—turning point. As noted earlier in this guide, the turning point is the point from which, especially in retrospect when we have reached the end of the story,

Macbeth begins the scene by refusing to "play the Roman fool and die / On mine own sword." To "play the Roman fool" is to commit suicide, so-called because of the practice of Roman officers to commit suicide to avoid the dishonor of defeat. For all the villainy of Macbeth, he shows a kind of superabundant, heroic energy in remaining combative to the end.

we can see how the action will be resolved. What
we learned at the turning point is that an external army is being formed that will defeat Macbeth.
But our engagement with events remains at a high
pitch during the further complication (which is
why the change of direction in the middle should
not be considered the climax). With the defeat of
Macbeth in battle we reach the climax of the plot,
immediately followed by the denouement.

The customary way for stories to end is with
poetic justice—that is, with good characters
rewarded and evil characters punished. Aristotle
even claimed that our moral sense is satisfied only if
such justice occurs. Tragedy is always based on the
premise of the tragic hero's being punished for his
tragic flaw of character as manifested in his tragic
choice, and that is what we witness in this scene.

The father of young Siward learns of his son's
death, and the father responds with a father's
pride in his son's courageous martial death. Older
civilizations, from classical antiquity through the
Renaissance, were in significant ways military
cultures that accepted what is often called the
heroic code—a set of values and virtues based on
the premise that success in battle was the highest goal a person could attain in life. Within this
value structure, particular emphasis was placed
on worthy sons. One can trace this motif from
Homer's *Odyssey* (where the ghost of Achilles in
the underworld marches away with pride when
he learns that his son had proved himself worthy
in battle) to the moment near the end of *Macbeth*
where Siward claims that he would not wish for
any son "a fairer death" than his son's heroic death
in battle. When Ross calls his son "God's soldier,"
we can also hear overtones of the "holy war" motif

Many editors assume
that the scene of
action shifts from
the battlefield to
inside Macbeth's
castle halfway through
scene 8, and some
editions even make
the concluding section
a separate scene.

in which a given war is viewed as a battle of God's followers against an evil force.

Macduff produces a sensational moment when he returns to the stage carrying the head of Macbeth atop a pole, to be displayed as a traitor's head. This, too, was a custom in heroic (military) cultures. The key line in Macduff's speech is, "The time is free," by which he means, "Our kingdom has been liberated in our time." Tragedies end with order reestablished, and this is achieved partly by Macduff's key statement.

Going all the way back to Greek tragedy, it is customary for literary tragedies to end on a note of closure and relief with the reestablishment of social and political order. Usually the king-to-be utters this speech. That is the convention at work in Malcolm's speech that ends the play. Malcolm vows to put an end to Macbeth's agents and to recall exiles who fled from Scotland during Macbeth's reign of terror. We also hear a final denunciation of Macbeth as "this dead butcher" and of Lady Macbeth as "his fiend-like queen" (accompanied by a reference to her death by suicide). Malcolm promises to set matters right "in measure, time, and place," conveying a firm sense of order, and he ends by inviting his allies to his coronation at Scone. In all of these ways we are led to feel that life has returned to a state of normalcy.

A specifically Christian note enters when Malcolm, amidst all the human plans he has in mind to reestablish order in the kingdom, acknowledges that he will accomplish all this "by the grace of Grace," a reference to divine providence. Obviously the capitalized "Grace" refers to the Christian God, so why didn't Shakespeare say God? A 1606 law in England had prohibited dramas from

It was a theatrical convention of Shakespeare's day that tragedies ended with a closing speech uttered by the person of highest rank who had survived the tragedy. Such speeches were formal-sounding and functioned as an epilogue to the play. Malcolm's speech at the end fits this rule of tragic composition.

mentioning God by name except in direct benediction, such as, "God be with him" (line 53 of this
scene). Virgil Whitaker comments regarding the
phrase "the grace of Grace" that "the phrase is an
obvious paraphrase of 'grace of God,' made necessary by the law of 1606, and it is Shakespeare's
clearest reference to man's dependence upon God's
co-operative grace sustaining him and working
with him if he is to do good works."

Alfred Harbage has this good comment on
the play's conclusion: "Thus ends this flawless
tragic poem. A great though simple truth has
been invested with tragic splendor. We feel that
we have been witnesses of the continuing creation
of moral law."

The Critics Comment on *Macbeth*

A good avenue toward unifying our experience of the play as a whole and reflecting on its deeper meanings is to ponder the following comments made by literary critics on Shakespeare's last great tragedy.

- "*Macbeth* is Shakespeare's most profound and mature vision of evil" (G. Wilson Knight).
- "*Macbeth* . . . presents the spectacle of a representative man and woman embarking on a sea of sin and error and encountering shipwreck" (Hardin Craig).
- "*Macbeth* is a study of immoral man in a moral universe" (Roy Walker).
- "The triumph of *Macbeth* is the construction of a world [that is] at once without and within Macbeth" (Mark Van Doren).
- "*Macbeth* is the tragedy of a man who, in full knowledge of what he was doing, destroyed his own soul. . . . *Macbeth* is the tragedy of every man who, neglecting the principles of morality and the voice of conscience, falls from the high estate for which he was destined into the slavery of sin" (Virgil K. Whitaker).
- "The theatre of the essential struggle is in Macbeth's mind. . . . Macbeth is his own antagonist, and fights a doomed battle not only against the world but against himself. . . . The simple central idea [is] that . . . there is no escape from conscience" (Donald Stauffer).
- "*Macbeth* is in many ways the most Christian of Shakespeare's plays" (Michael Long).
- "The great idea of *Macbeth*, uttered in the first few scenes with a tragic energy which has never been equaled . . . , is the idea of the enormous mistake a man makes if he supposes that one decisive act will clear his way. . . . The second idea in the main story of *Macbeth* is . . . the influence of evil suggestion upon the soul" (G. K. Chesterton).
- "Its action is simply the yielding of a great and good man to temptation and the degeneration of his moral nature resulting from his first deed of sin. . . . The theme of *Macbeth* is therefore the causes and consequences of human sin, of which the story of Macbeth is an *exemplum*. This theme dominates the entire play" (Virgil K. Whitaker).

Further Resources

Virtually any current edition of Shakespeare's plays will give an accurate version of the text. This extends to both paperback versions and copies of the play that appear in collected works of Shakespeare's plays. Paperback versions have the advantage of being more portable, and they are less cluttered with footnotes than scholarly editions of the complete works usually are. All editions are likely to have good introductions to the play, and these should usually be regarded as a good repository of literary criticism on the play. The Catholic-affiliated Ignatius Press has an edition of the play (Joseph Pearce, editor) with critical essays that speak to Christian implications of the play from a Catholic perspective.

Like other Shakespearean plays, *Macbeth* has appeared in audio version for many years. A library is a likely source for audio versions. Several good film versions of *Macbeth* are readily available, though others are less good because they accentuate the violence too much or are so experimental as to be a departure from anything that Shakespeare could possibly have intended. If a choice exists, pick one of the following three (or choose more than one and compare the differing interpretations and effects): (a) a Thames Video Collection/HBO Video version starring Michael Jayston and Barbara Leigh Hunt in the lead roles; (b) a Crest Video Marketing version featuring Jeremy Brett and Piper Laurie; (c) a British Broadcasting Company (BBC) version starring Nicol Williamson and Jane Lapotaire.

In addition to the books on *Macbeth* listed below, it is worth noting the extreme usefulness of a book on Shakespeare and his plays generally: Norrie Epstein, *The Friendly Shakespeare* (New York: Viking, 1993). Another goldmine of information on all the plays is Andrew Dickson, *The Rough Guide to Shakespeare* (London: Rough Guides, 2005, 2009). Some of the following books have chapters on *Macbeth* along with chapters on other Shakespearean tragedies.

Bloom, Harold, ed. *Macbeth*. Major Literary Characters Series. New York: Chelsea House, 1991.

———, ed. *William Shakespeare's Macbeth*. Modern Critical Interpretations Series. New York: Chelsea House, 1987.

Coursen, H. R. *Macbeth: A Guide to the Play*. Westport, CT: Greenwood, 1997.

Harbage, Alfred. *William Shakespeare: A Reader's Guide*. New York: Farrar, Straus, 1963.

Hawkes, Terrence, ed. *Twentieth Century Interpretations of Macbeth*. Englewood Cliffs, NJ: Prentice Hall, 1977.
Excellent but out of print.

Jack, Jane H. "*Macbeth*, King James, and the Bible." *English Literary History* 22 (1955): 173–93.
Focuses on the biblical presence in the play, including the moral pattern of Old Testament chronicles and the apocalyptic imagery of the New Testament book of Revelation.

Jorgensen, Paul A. *Our Naked Frailties: Sensational Art and Meaning in Macbeth*. Berkeley: University of California Press, 1971.
Especially good on the religious meanings of the play's imagery, primarily in regard to the moral drama of temptation, crime, and punishment.

Long, Michael. *Macbeth*. Twayne's New Critical Introductions to Shakespeare Series. Boston: G. K. Hall, 1989.
One of the best overviews of leading issues and of the history of criticism on the play.

Ribner, Irving. *Patterns in Shakespearian Tragedy*. London: Methuen, 1960.
Moral patterns in the tragedies.

Rosenberg, Marvin. *The Masks of Macbeth*. Newark, DE: University of Delaware Press, 1978.
Scene-by-scene information about the play in performance.

Ryken, Leland. "Shakespeare and the Bible." In *Word and Rite: The Bible and Ceremony in Selected Shakespearean Works*, chap. 1. Edited by Beatrice Batson. Newcastle upon Tyne: Cambridge Scholars Publishing, 2010.
Uses *Macbeth* to illustrate generalizations about Shakespeare's use of the Bible.

———. "Shakespeare's *Macbeth* and the Tragic Spirit in Literature." *Realms of Gold: The Classics in Christian Perspective*, chap. 3. Wheaton, IL: Harold Shaw, 1991.

Schoenbaum, S. *Macbeth: Critical Essays*. New York: Garland, 1991.

Wilson, Harold S. *On the Design of Shakespearian Tragedy*. Toronto: University of Toronto Press, 1957.
Christian patterns in the tragedies.

Whitaker, Virgil K. *The Mirror up to Nature: The Technique of Shakespeare's Tragedies*. San Marino, CA: Huntington Library, 1965.
Good general commentary.

Glossary of Literary Terms Used in This Book

Allusion. A reference to past history or literature.

Archetype. A plot motif (such as the quest), character type (such as the villain), or image or setting (e.g., darkness) that recurs throughout literature and life.

Dramatic irony. A situation in which the reader knows something that one or more characters in the work of literature do not know.

Foil. Anything in a story (e.g., a character, plotline, or setting) that *sets off* something in the main story by being either a parallel or a contrast.

Genre. Literary type or kind, such as story or poem.

Imagery. An image is any word that names an object or action. Imagery is the collection of images in a work. Often it is used to denote an image pattern—a string of occurrences of the same image, such as light imagery.

Subtext. An episode or complete story from an older text on which an author constructs a passage; the earlier work underlies the later one and serves as a model as the author composes.

Well-made plot. A framework that modern literary criticism devised to show the pattern and unity in a carefully constructed story. The well-made plot unfolds in the following order: exposition (explaining the ingredients that make the story possible); inciting moment or inciting force (the thing that begins the action or plot conflict); rising action; turning point (the point that signals how the plot conflict(s) will eventually be resolved); further complication; climax; denouement (tying up of loose ends).